To Elizabeth,
Shalom!
Rosie

Heart to Heart
with Rosie Boom

Boom Tree Publishing

What readers are saying...

'Having had the honour to sit at Rosie's feet for many a HEART conference, I am thrilled to see that this book has now brought together so many of her teaching, tips, insights and encouragements. These have been manna to many a hungry soul over the years. This book brings exactly the same feeling of sitting listening to Rosie. The pages ring with her cheerful voice, beautiful smile and contagious laughter! Whether you are new to homeschooling, or have been on the marathon for a while, you will find refreshment, encouragement and plenty of practical advice between these pages. Listening to Rosie (and others) at HEART conferences over the years has been the best thing I could find for my professional development as a home educator. Now there's no need to wait until the next big event! Grab a cuppa, find a quiet corner (!) and delve into this wonderful book. You need never feel like you are alone on this wonderful, but sometimes hard, journey of educating your children. I highly recommend this eagerly awaited book, filled with wisdom from Rosie – a wonderful wife, mother and legendary home educator here in NZ.'

—Sheena Harris

'Just what I need as I begin to think about homeschooling!'

—Monica

'In the chapters of this book you will find words of encouragement from a true champion and cheerleader of homeschooling. Rosie offers, from years of experience, the type of insight and hope that every homeschooling mama needs, and her words pour over one's heart like a precious balm.'

—Janice

'It's a wonderful thing to glean knowledge from someone further ahead in the journey than you. Reading this book is like you're having a conversation over a cup of tea with Rosie. She shares her experience of homeschooling her children and offers us her wealth of wisdom, inspiration, practical tips and encouragement while always pointing us to Jesus, the one who gave it all. Thank you for sharing your wisdom with us, Rosie, to continue on or to start our own homeschooling journey. Your book is so encouraging and inspiring! What a way to end the school year and feel encouraged and brave to do it all again next year.'

—Rachel

AUDITING THE DATA PROCESSING FUNCTION

Richard W. Lott

amacom
A Division of
American Management Associations

Library of Congress Cataloging in Publication Data

Lott, Richard W
  Auditing the data processing function.

  Bibliography: p.
  Includes index.
  1. Electronic data processing departments—
Auditing. I. Title.
HF5548.2.L599   658'.05'4   79-54841
ISBN 0-8144-5527-1

© 1980 AMACOM
A division of American Management Associations, New York.
All rights reserved. Printed in the United States of America.

This publication may not be reproduced, stored in a retrieval system, or transmitted in whole or in part, in any form or by any means, electronic, mechanical, photocopying, recording, or otherwise, without the prior written permission of AMACOM, 135 West 50th Street, New York, N.Y. 10020.

First Printing

Preface

This book has been written for a variety of users. Major attention is devoted to managers charged with the responsibility of guiding the organization, whatever its nature may be. The thrust to management focuses on the risks inherent in the use of computers and what can be done to minimize those risks within cost-effective limits.

For data processing management, there are ideas as to what both upper management and auditors are looking for in a data processing operation. Both latter groups are going to continue to get more involved in the work of their data processors and to expect more tangible results from them.

Relevant ideas are offered for those who are now auditors and those who plan to become auditors. Since this book is not intended to be the last word on all aspects of a data processing audit, an aspiring auditor will need to obtain substantial amounts of additional education. In any event, the approach taken here is to provide a discussion of the major issues rather than a complete checklist for an EDP audit.

Finally, this material should be of interest to the wide range of users of data processing services. My objective is to help users proceed to a point where they can see and appreciate problems and deficiencies and then recommend changes that will improve their systems enough to make a substantial effect on the bottom line.

In recent years, we have seen plenty of evidence of improperly designed and poorly operated systems. It might be well to carefully study such failures and learn as much from them as we can. Although there are efforts in many organizations to educate employees in the data processing area, the focus of that education usually is on the technical details of computers and programming. But those aren't the major stumbling blocks to the more effective use of computers; it is not surprising, then, that many users who have undergone such technically oriented training continue to make the same types of mistakes. I have tried to help in that area by concentrating on the major areas that need attention by all parties concerned.

The plan of this book is to take the data processing function and break it down into five major segments, ranging from preinstallation to actual operation. Each of these five segments is discussed in a separate chapter, which suggests some appropriate goals for that segment; describes the major functions involved; suggests some standards for the activity; describes relevant documentation; details the major controls that are appropriate; and then shows how to go about auditing that segment.

Separate sections provide an annotated bibliography of the outstanding literature in this field and a glossary of important data processing terms.

It should be emphasized that this book was written for the person who does not have a strong technical background in computer data processing. The use of technical jargon has been minimized, and many of the operating details have been avoided.

Richard W. Lott

Contents

1 Computers and Auditing 1
2 Preinstallation Activities 33
3 System Development 67
4 Computer Program Development 94
5 Raw Data Generation and Data Conversion 128
6 Computer Center Operations 155
7 Other Issues 185
   Glossary 193
   Supplementary Readings 199
   Index 203

1

Computers and Auditing

Mechanized data processing systems have been in use since about 1895. It was then that Herman Hollerith, an employee of the U.S. Census Bureau, invented equipment that would help process census data. Shortly afterward, large businesses began to use such equipment to eliminate clerical functions on accounts payable, billing, and payroll applications. Hollerith eventually formed a company that was the predecessor of International Business Machines Corporation (IBM).

Despite a start so long ago, it wasn't until the late 1950s that computers came into their own as popular devices for processing business applications. At first, computers were used to perform a few simple steps that previously had been handled by people. But times are changing quickly. Computers are now used to do more than just a few incidental steps in an overall process. A computer can accept a source transaction such as a customer order; check the customer's credit; prepare a shipping order; prepare an invoice; update inventory, accounts-receivable, and sales-analysis records; and reorder inventory. Computers are being used to initiate transactions without any help from people, such as preparing a purchase order to a vendor.

2 AUDITING THE DATA PROCESSING FUNCTION

In the typical organization, computer activities very likely were permitted to go their own way, without much supervision, for several years early in their existence. This lack of proper supervision, made possible by a certain mystique surrounding computers, no doubt contributed to excessive costs and a level of service far below that expected by users and promised by data processing specialists. Some of that early computer mystique is now wearing off, partly thanks to the availability of sound courses in computer concepts geared to managers and other users. Organizations now recognize that they can manage data processing departments just as they can manage any other segment of operation. They are beginning to require, not just expect, healthy contributions from computer activities, just as they do from other units.

The most effective way for an organization to get managerial control over the computer is to audit all phases of its operation. Indeed, we are quickly moving into an era where all computer centers can expect to be audited on a continuing basis. The major obstacle to effective EDP auditing today is the very complexity of computer applications. In the past, it was possible to review, or audit, any operation that involved a computer simply by checking manually prepared input and computer output as well as subsequent uses of such output. Thus it was possible for an auditor to certify a firm's financial statements, for example, without paying much attention to the computer itself. Today, a comparable audit could not be performed without detailed consideration of the computer systems and programs used in generating the financial data. In view of the pervasive use of the computer in business, then, EDP auditing must be expected to become a central part of the general auditing process.

THE PROBLEM

Reading the current literature and listening to the pleas of many speakers, one receives the general impression that control of data processing is either poor or altogether lacking.

Some of the critical reports come as a result of an audit; the more exciting ones generate a great deal of publicity because embarrassing details are allowed to get outside the organization. But those who criticize organizations for failing to control their data processing operations tend to ignore the fact that control costs money. Every control step put in requires some effort that usually takes away from employees' time available to do their regular work. In some cases an organization, after making a careful study of the situation, may decide that it cannot justify the cost of putting a control into operation.

For example, in 1978 a bank reported that, due to a keypunching error, it had credited two $50,000 deposits of a corporation to an individual's account. When the individual found out the money was in his account, he withdrew all of it and skipped town. An obvious control appropriate at a bank is to constantly check accounts for any unusual activity. Since that control is extremely common and surely must have come to the attention of all bankers, it seems safe to conclude that this particular bank, after studying the costs and benefits of the control, deliberately chose not to add it to its system.

Another reason, besides cost-benefit considerations, why an automated system may lack important controls is the sales pitch used by some equipment vendors. Salesmen's comments about how automatic the computer is ("You never have to worry about that") may be taken at face value and trusted far too much, leading to the belief that system design is an easy matter and requires no special controls. But trouble often arises later; by then it is usually deemed too costly or just not worth the effort to go back and redesign the system. Thus there are many poorly controlled systems, some of which have caused serious damage.

Another cause of poor control relates to who is responsible for the system design. If computer specialists are allowed to design a system, perhaps without much input from users or auditors, essential controls may be left out. Computer specialists may be more concerned with getting the job out quickly or using an exotic method to solve a problem. They may not understand or care about controls enough to include them. Because of the way a programming language is designed, one of the controls they probably do use is concerned with checking input for valid characters (otherwise, the computer can't accept the data and won't run the job at all). On the other hand, there may be no programmed check at all to determine if a given dollar amount is reasonable.

One consequence of poor or nonexisting controls is that financial and other reports about operations are inadequate or untimely, in turn causing poor decisions. For example, a manufacturing company consistently found that its physical inventory was about $100,000 short of its book inventory each year. This had happened so often that top management had come to accept the shortage as normal. Then one year the physical inventory was higher than the book inventory by $100,000. Alarmed by this unexpected excess inventory, management at last decided to look into the situation. The reason for the discrepancies, it turned out, was that the company had poor control over returns from customers.

Another, less obvious consequence is that audit costs will increase, for if an auditor detects poor control, he will naturally be concerned about the accuracy of the system and insist on auditing the data more extensively. And, of course, poor control always has the potential of exposing an operation to fraud.

Should all controls be cost-effective? That is a difficult question to answer. Whereas the cost of a control can often be readily estimated, the benefits frequently cannot. In many cases, the best that can be done is to estimate the magnitude of the most likely benefit and make a decision based on that. There are situations, however, when even that seems out of the question. Yet it makes good sense to provide a control.

Of course, some care must be taken to make sure that controls aren't overdone. For example, when preparing to enter the personal data for new employees into the employee master file, a company chose to both visually and key-verify the data prior to entry. When that same company proceeded to computerize the names and addresses of potential customers for direct mail advertising, it continued to apply both verification methods. Eventually management took a look at the situation, and concluded that in this latter case, controls were being overdone. The reasoning was that it would require a serious error to prevent the mail from being delivered to the right person, and it was further felt that recipients were unlikely to be seriously offended if an error had been made in the spelling of either name or address.

A careful assessment has to be made about the potential impact of legal requirements. For example, Congress passed the Foreign Corrupt Practices Act of 1977. While the bill got its name from its antibribery provisions, it has requirements that are not all related to a firm's foreign operations. For our purposes here, the essential features are the maintenance of a system of internal control that will assure that

1. Transactions are executed according to management authorization.
2. The system will provide for the preparation of financial statements and the accountability of assets.
3. Access to assets is in accordance with management authorization.
4. Book assets are reconciled to physical assets at reasonable intervals.

The Institute of Internal Auditors (IIA) has become heavily involved with control and audit topics as related to computers. Aided by a $500,000 grant from IBM, the institute commissioned SRI International (formerly Stanford Research Institute) to conduct a major study of EDP audit problems. This three-volume report, entitled Systems Auditability and Control (SAC) was published in 1977 by IIA. The major conclusions of the report were:

Control and audit practices have not kept up with the pace of EDP development.
Audit specialists and computer specialists have not coordinated their activities as well as they might or should have for the benefit of the employer.

Auditors do not seem to be well equipped to perform their duties with respect to computerized operations. Top management has not given proper attention to the problem of EDP control and has not made a clear mandate to auditors.

Much of the material in the SAC report was based either on interviews with computer users or on questionnaires. It was the opinion of those polled that most losses are due to honest errors and omissions, which in turn are primarily caused by inadequate system design. This book will, therefore, concentrate on those topics.

The report also identifies 28 audit techniques. Each of them is described in the report in terms of what it does, how it does it, and its feasibility and potential usefulness. A number of the techniques described, however, currently seem little more than theories with negligible practical applicability, and therefore will not be dealt with in this book. Furthermore, some techniques will be discussed that were not considered in the IIA-sponsored report. An example is the use of physical observation with an occasional surprise visit.

TYPES OF EDP AUDITS

Audits of EDP activities can be broken down into four categories:

1. External audit by a CPA firm. This audit is generally performed to gather evdence that will help the CPA firm to express an opinion on the organization's published financial statements. Since so many of the client's finance-related systems are computerized, it is necessary to study the computer and to see how those systems work. Such an external audit may also be concerned with internal control and the protection of organization assets. These latter audit objectives can normally be met much more effectively by auditing the system rather than only data.

2. External audit by a taxing body, such as the IRS, or by an

industry watchdog, such as the state banking or insurance examiner. The purpose of this type of audit is somewhat similar to that of the CPA audit. Since the client has released certain financial information, and since many customers of the business are continuing to rely upon its continuing operation, the audit is performed to make sure the company has what it says it has. Again, some of the emphasis is upon internal control to make sure that assets are protected.

3. External audit by a taxing body, such as the IRS. The IRS is certainly concerned about the accuracy of the calculation of the income tax liability. The IRS relies heavily upon the taxpayer's retention of accounting data in a computer-processable form.

4. Internal audit by specially designated employees (internal auditors or EDP auditors) or by external auditing experts hired on a short-term basis. The purpose of this type of audit could be any of the following:

○ Ensure accuracy (relative freedom from error) in all phases of the operation. This is directly related to internal control and overall protection of assets. Hopefully, greater accuracy will help produce better results.
○ Check the effectiveness of the system. Are users getting what they need or were led to believe they would get?
○ Ensure the efficiency of the system, or its cost-effective use of resources. Efficiency and effectiveness are not to be considered the same. A system may deliver valuable results (be effective), but at an unjustifiable cost (that is, inefficiently). On the other hand, a system may operate efficiently, or at low cost, but produce results of no great value.
○ Make sure prescribed policies and procedures are being followed. Systems are designed to operate in specific ways, and the audit is a method to check if they do. For example, a system may have been designed to follow a specific set of steps in developing a credit rating for a new customer or changing the rating of an existing customer. In the course of an internal audit, it may be found that this

prescribed procedure has inadvertently been altered, say, because of day-to-day operating problems. (This aspect of the audit may involve certain legal requirements that need to be carefully watched.)
- Conduct performance reviews. These could be used to establish employee error levels, detect inefficiencies or bottlenecks, or identify quality work for the purpose of promotion or merit increases.
- Prevent fraud. Much more will be said about this topic later.
- Protect privacy. With all the current attitudes and laws regarding the invasion of privacy, it may be necessary to audit the system to determine if it adheres to the law.
- Protect proprietary data and/or programs. Management most likely wants to have a periodic check on security measures for data and programs to ensure they don't get in the hands of competitors or anyone else who could use them to the detriment of the owner.
- Ensure security of people, data, programs, and hardware. Here we are concerned about the methods used to prevent loss or destruction due to fire, flood, and other such events that could seriously hamper the ability of a computer system to continue to operate effectively. A major consideration is the ability to recover from losses should they occur.
- Any other item management or the internal auditor wants to check.

Much of an internal auditor's work could have a significant impact upon any external audit that is to be performed in the same time period. A well-executed internal audit can be very useful to an external auditor and may indeed help reduce the costs of an external audit by a significant amount. Also, the internal audit, being practically oriented, may lead to helpful suggestions for improving operations.

In this book we will look at EDP auditing from the broader standpoint of an internal auditor. However, the principles discussed should have general applicability, since there is significant overlap between both the methods and the purposes of

Figure 1. Summary of the interests of various auditing groups.

	CPA	IRS	Government Agency	Internal Audit
Accuracy	H	H	H	H
Effectiveness	M	-	M	H
Efficiency	M	-	-	H
Following policies and procedures	H	M	M	H
Performance review	-	-	-	H
Fraud	M	-	M	H
Privacy	-	M	M	H
Proprietary nature	-	-	-	H
Security	M	M	M	H

H = High interest M = Moderate interest - = Little or no direct interest

different types of audits. Figure 1 summarizes the concerns of the four different groups of auditors.

THE WHAT OF AN EDP AUDIT

Although it is generally helpful to find out what others are doing when one is about to initiate a process, I think it is desirable to spend a little time thinking independently about how one intends to proceed. I will therefore temporarily put myself in the position of an owner of a business or that of a manager who has been hired to run a business.

What, then, would I want my internal EDP auditor to do? I think I would want the auditor to come back eventually and tell me either that everything is reasonably all right or what's wrong and what should be done to correct the trouble spots.

Where would I want my auditor to look? In principle, at all major segments of the EDP operation. Since that covers a great number of topics, however, I would expect immediate attention to only certain aspects, with the plan that all items eventually be reviewed. I would certainly like to have the chance to be directly involved in establishing the relative priority of the areas to be reviewed.

Just what are those major areas? For the sake of convenience, I have broken the overall EDP operation into the following five segments:

1. Preinstallation activities.
2. System development.
3. Computer program development.
4. Raw data generation and data conversion.
5. Computer center operations.

Although some authors may break those segments into greater detail and end up with anywhere from seven to twelve segments, this classification does include all essential activities. Each of the five areas will be discussed in a separate chapter, in the order stated.

Of the various items an auditor may be concerned about, we will focus on just five, namely, accuracy, efficiency, fraud prevention, security, and effectiveness. There will be a certain amount of overlap among those items. A brief introduction to each of the five topics follows.

Accuracy

A student of mine reported an interesting aspect of an EDP operation at the company where he worked. The firm's part-time workers were required to prepare a time sheet for each week. In a recent pay period, the student worked only half a

COMPUTERS AND AUDITING 11

day, for which he properly prepared the time sheet. He signed the form, which was duly approved by the department supervisor and sent on to the timekeeping department. There a clerk determined the hours worked per day, added the daily figures to get a total for the week, and then wrote the total in the appropriate box on the form. Unfortunately, the clerk entered 40 hours instead of 4 hours in the total box, and the form was sent along with all other time sheets to the keypunch department. There the data were keypunched onto cards, and the cards were key-verified and went on to the computer for payroll preparation. How much did the employee get paid? As might be guessed, he was paid for 40 hours. This simple example points out that:

- While some errors are self-correcting due to such things as employee or customer complaints, this one was not: the employee did not complain.
- All the key verification in the world does not catch errors that exist in source data. Neither does a control such as a batch total. Great care must be taken to install appropriate controls to ensure that source data are accurate.
- Controls need to be devised to check on all aspects of EDP operations; this means not only the specific steps within the computer center but also the manual steps that precede or succeed EDP.

As previously mentioned, most control problems relate to plain, ordinary, everyday, run-of-the-mill errors. It is one thing to deal with those errors by finding them and correcting them. It is quite another to determine what causes them and to try to design a system in a fashion that will prevent them or minimize their impact.

What causes all these "honest" errors? A partial list would include the following causes:

Poorly designed input forms.
Lack of instruction and training.
Workload pressures and deadlines.

Poor review or no review by supervisors.
Poor handwriting by those doing the recording.
Boredom.
An "I don't care" attitude.

As this list suggests, an audit must consider many different aspects of an operation, and it must look not only at results but at causes as well. Important as the quantitative aspects of a problem are, to be effective, an audit must carefully consider the human side as well.

Also, it is not enough to determine that a system is ultimately accurate and stop there. For example, an audit of a payroll system may prove that paychecks are highly accurate. This does not mean that the overall system is acceptable. We have to carefully consider how much it cost to get that accuracy. How many errors were caught and corrected? While it is commendable to catch and correct errors, the cost may have been too high. There may have been too much emphasis on error detection and correction and not enough emphasis on prevention. Perhaps alternative control methods, such as designing better source documents, a better training program, or better employee selection techniques, may prove to be much more cost-effective ways of preventing errors than key verification and the rekeying of needed corrections.

Efficiency

Consider the following situation. A computer center employee is operating the computer in the middle of a four-hour run, when the company president calls and wants a special job run immediately. Short of overruling or ignoring the president's request, the operator stops the present job, runs the president's report, and then restarts the other job from the beginning, since end-of-job totals are a critical part of the job. How can such inefficiency be prevented?

The name of the programming technique to use here is a *checkpoint*. A checkpoint is simply a periodic computer procedure, effected through programming, that establishes certain reference points by saving relevant totals. It permits you to restart a program from the last checkpoint rather than from the beginning. It is a good idea to establish checkpoints in all programs that run more than thirty minutes or so.

Note that an auditor would have to be quite skillful, if not plain lucky, to come across a situation such as that described above unless it happened on a regular basis. Possibly, a detailed review of the operators' log sheets would turn up the problem. In general, however, one of the surest and most cost-effective ways to correct inefficiencies is to establish a relationship of trust between the auditor and the employees charged with various phases of the EDP operaton. For instance, if the EDP operator in our example approached the internal auditor (assuming there is one), reported the situation to him, and simply asked how such waste could be avoided, much time that would otherwise have to be spent on system analysis could be saved.

The issue of computer center efficiency deserves a great deal of attention, because computer centers seem particularly prone to inefficiencies. Reasons for this are, among others:

- Computer center managers are more frequently competent technicians than they are effective managers.
- There is a natural incentive to overexpand the data processing department, and this tendency is more difficult to control in a technical area such as EDP than in less technical areas, which are more accessible to upper management.
- Top management tends to do a poor job at managing computer specialists.
- Audits of computer centers are relatively new and untried.

Here are some examples of items that an auditor might look for:

- Specific pieces of computer equipment that have a low usage rate. Perhaps the equipment was obtained for one specific job, but it then is idle the rest of the time.

14 AUDITING THE DATA PROCESSING FUNCTION

- Running a job several times to obtain multi-copy reports. Studies usually show it is more efficient to run through the computer just once and then to use a copying process.
- The level of computer reruns. These can usually be reduced by carefully analyzing the causes and solving problems at the source.

Fraud Prevention

One of the more difficult tasks of an auditor is to decide how much emphasis to place on the prevention and detection of computer fraud. The topic of computer fraud receives a great deal of press coverage, and fraud case studies are usually much more exciting to readers than most other computer topics.

It appears that traditionally, in regular assignments, external auditors want to avoid the responsibility for detecting fraud. One reason is that the fee they earn for expressing an opinion on financial statements is not great enough to cover the additional effort needed to look for fraud. Another reason is that auditors are reluctant to sign a statement certifying that there is no fraud present. In most of the cases where fraud was detected after auditors had certified the statements and management or owners had sued the auditors for not finding the fraud, judgment has not gone against the auditors except in the most unusual situations. The detection of fraud will thus generally be the responsibility of internal auditors or external auditors who have specifically taken on such a job.

Figure 2 shows an example of a program flowchart with fraudulent logic. The program calculates an employee's pay and the total wages paid by the firm, counts the number of employees, and prints a pay register. But before a check is to be printed, a test determines whether the check is for John Doe; if it is, the check is printed for $10,000 (or whatever amount the programmer wants). The count of employees and the total pay are printed at the end of the job.

The example is not to suggest that John Doe would leave such documentation lying around; the chart merely shows the logical approach a programmer might take if he intended to

Figure 2. Program flowchart with fraudulent logic.

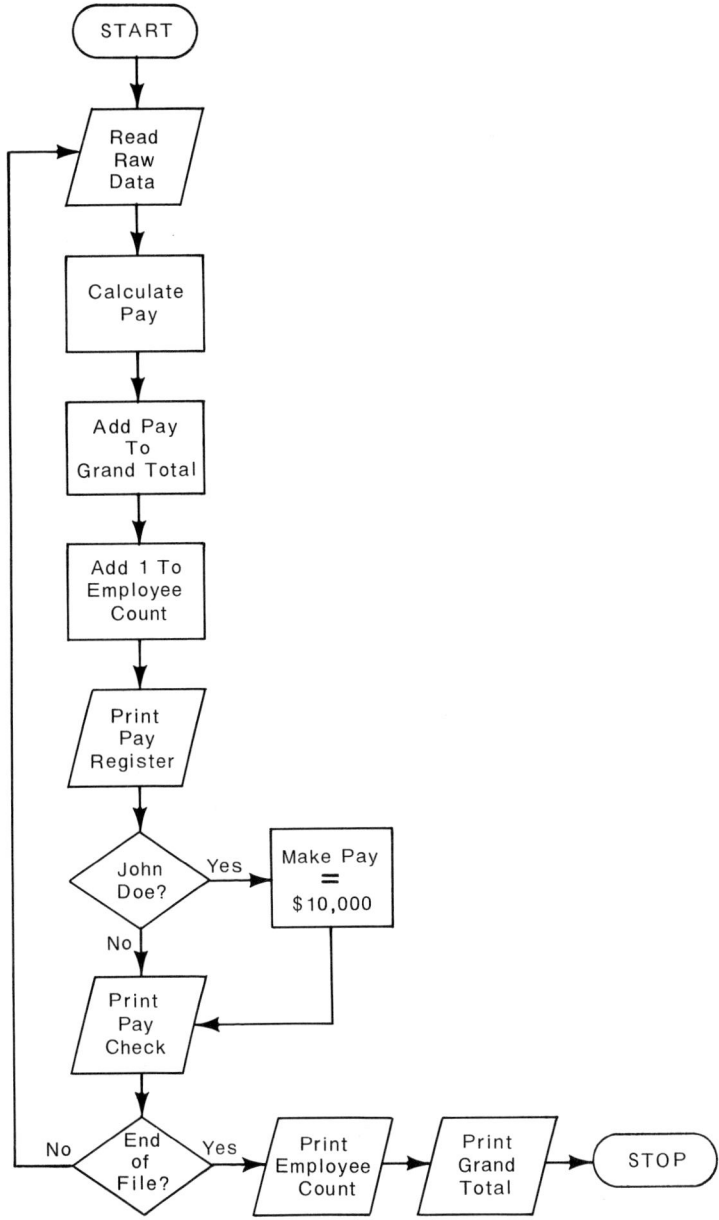

defraud his employer. I have shown this diagram to hundreds of people in courses, speeches, and informal discussions. The chart has caused comments such as:

> Would it really be that easy for a programmer to steal from an employer?
> At my company, a programmer couldn't get away with that because:
> The boss signs all the checks.
> The books wouldn't balance.
> The payroll account would be overdrawn.
> We are bonded against such losses.
> Our programmers can't go into the computer room.
> We reconcile the account every month and would catch the thief then.
> We hire only honest people.

It is, perhaps unfortunately, true that it would be that easy for a programmer to insert fraudulent steps into a program. Since programmers must have available a wide variety of possible steps needed to perform the acceptable functions, it becomes difficult to prevent them from inserting whatever they choose. Thus it is necessary to create an environment that discourages programmers from committing fraud and, secondly, that allows prompt discovery of fraud.

Some comments are appropriate to the statements that various controls would catch such an act. Even if a manager does sign all the checks, that process can become quite boring, with the result that the person may look less critically at the amounts. Furthermore, if the hypothetical John Doe should make the check for a more reasonable amount than $10,000, the manager would be unlikely to catch that on a routine review. Finally, if the payroll is computerized, that suggests a certain volume of checks which in the near future are likely to be mechanically signed.

If the computer run shown in Figure 2 becomes the basis for the amount of money to be paid and the money is in fact paid, that doesn't necessarily mean the books would not balance.

However, if a good budgeting and cost-charging system is used, an abnormal expense may be noticed. The same applies to the suggestion that the payroll account would be overdrawn. While bonding may be a means to recover from such a loss, bonding is usually considered a last resort. It is normally better to spend reasonable effort to prevent the need to apply for relief from a bonding company.

Note also that to commit this type of fraud does not require that the programmer ever enter the computer center. To apply the technique, the programmer would need only to write the applicable steps and then wait for the checks to arrive.

A reconciliation may or may not catch the thief. Does the person reconciling an account look at the amounts that closely? Furthermore, if the programmer chose to get a large check on a one-time basis and then disappear, the reconciliation method would be too late.

Given the potential financial impact of fraud, it is certainly wise to devote some time and energy to preventive measures. It is desirable to do some research on fraud to determine the types that have taken place. This is not to say that those types will necessarily be the ones to continue to prevail, but history does tend to repeat itself. Once you have seen what has already happened, you may be in a better position to anticipate fraudulent schemes that someone may try in the future.

In addition to studying actual types of fraud, it may be helpful to conduct brainstorming sessions with the aim of generating new schemes that might conceivably be used by fraud perpetrators.

Having identified potential fraud opportunities, management is in a better position to decide what should be done about them. As a first step, the various potential threats may be put into categories of ease, or likelihood of happening. Next, for each type of threat, management should decide how much it is willing to spend on prevention or detection. Clearly, the amount spent must be in a sensible relationship to the potential financial loss that is to be prevented. Finally, appropriate methods of protection must be selected, within the financial limits established. Figure 3 shows a simple decision matrix that

Figure 3. A decision matrix for developing a fraud-prevention strategy.

Likelihood of Occurrence	Financial Impact		
	High	Medium	Low
High			
Medium			
Low			

might be used to facilitate the task. Fraud types that fall in the *high financial impact/high likelihood of occurrence* cell in this matrix would be candidates for the most expensive forms of protection, whereas threats assigned to the *low impact/low likelihood* cell would not justify any significant expenditures. Such an approach, incidentally, may prove useful in considering controls in general, whether they relate to fraud, security, accuracy, or efficiency.

There are some factors that may attract fraud or at least make it easier to commit. Some examples are:

Lack of separation of duties.
Lack of job rotation.
Ease of access to various parts of the system.
Knowledge that the system is poorly controlled or that apprehension will have no serious consequences.
Ineffective auditing.
Management's unawareness of exposure to fraud.

A comment on job rotation is in order. When people are rotated from one job to another, particularly with a short notice given as to when the shift will take place, they are presumably less inclined to commit fraudulent acts because of the fear of being caught. On the other hand, job rotation creates a potential danger. As a person becomes familiar with a whole operation, he or she may observe potential or actual weak spots. Hopefully the benefits of job rotation outweigh the risks.

A company in the coffee-and-doughnut business decided to install cameras that would take pictures of all cash register transactions. As soon as the cameras started into operation, "sales" went up 20 percent with no corresponding increase in the number of doughnuts that had to be manufactured. What the employees needed was to see that management intended to put in a strict control. As soon as it was there, the employees quit their act.

Incidentally, an acquaintance of mine, hearing of this incident, started manufacturing a cameralike device that had a "lens" and a blinking light. At last report he was doing a brisk business selling this "detector" to businesses that wanted a gadget that looked like a control.

If managers and auditors will only recognize the broad potential exposure to fraud, then appropriate efforts can be made to keep fraudulent activities within acceptable limits. Throughout the book I will try to keep from concentrating on fraud, as easy as it would be to repeat all the interesting cases.

Security

The topic of security relates to procedures whose objectives are to assure that equipment, programs, and data are kept safe so that they are available for use when needed. The major specific hazards to be guarded against are fire, flood, employee error, civil disruption, and disgruntled employees. In a broader sense, one would be concerned about humidity and temperature controls, power supplies, and access by people. Not surprisingly, prevention of improper access generally presents greater problems than protection against natural hazards. In the case of one computer center which tried to be a good neighbor by providing public tours within the center, a visitor pulled and retained one punched card from a card deck sitting next to the computer. That particular card represented a significant step in a complex program. When that program was to be run the next time, it took two hours of searching to identify the missing card and replace it.

Some computer users have experienced almost equally undesirable results from letting employees into the computer room. At the least, their presence caused disruption in computer room operations. The current trend is to provide access only to those who need to be in the computer room to perform their job duties—generally only computer operators and perhaps keypunch operators and control clerks. In many cases, programmers are denied access.

Effectiveness

Overall effectiveness is involved with doing the right things the right way. Putting it another way, there must be a way to see if EDP is producing the results that help its various user departments do their jobs. A common complaint I hear is that people get many reports they don't need but not enough of the reports they do need.

In line with a comment made earlier, possibly the greatest effort should be placed on protecting against honest day-to-day errors that are likely to be made by people, namely, errors in creating programs, errors in creating data, and errors in operating the equipment. Each of these points must be properly controlled so that EDP can provide accurate and timely services. It naturally follows that an audit is periodically required to ensure that the system is working reasonably well.

An audit can be used not only to determine if things are being done right but also to make sure the right things are being done. To handle this latter aspect of EDP, both users and auditors must get more involved in the initial process of system design; once a system is installed, getting it to perform needed tasks ignored during the original design usually involves a major redesign effort.

STANDARDS

A large part of this book deals with standards. The term will be used in either of two ways. Which meaning is intended in a specific case should be clear from the context in which it is used. In the first sense, a standard is a *guide to a uniform procedure*. In this context, a standard may specify a certain way to perform any step that needs to be repeated many times. The use of standards may lead to specialization and simpler training procedures, in turn making possible significant savings. A possible negative consequence of such use of standards is that it may stifle creativity; new methods may not be used or even considered even when they would be better than the standard itself. Examples of procedural standards are:

All flowcharts are to use the following symbols only [show a list of them] and are always to begin in the upper left side of the page and flow down and to the right.

All programs will be written either in FORTRAN or in COBOL. Any exceptions to this rule are to be cleared with the Programming Manager.

All employees in the department will be evaluated by filling out Form 193, attaching documents that show relevant performance in the last six months, and then meeting with the supervisor and the proper member of the Personnel Department.

In the second sense, a standard is a *yardstick for measuring performance*. To be useful, such performance measures generally should be quantitative. Examples are:

Keypunch operators are to attain a minimum recording rate of 8,000 characters per hour with errors being properly considered (after having provided for the correction of errors once detected by any later verification process).

All work is to be completed in a time no more than 5 percent longer than that originally quoted to the customer. Any job that exceeds the 5 percent variance is to be reported and justified to management.

The computer cannot be permitted to be down for more than ten minutes at a time nor more than five times a month.

The Need for EDP Auditing Standards

It is not difficult to make a case for the need to develop EDP auditing standards. We need sets of yardstick standards so that an auditor can determine if what he has found is good or not. The use of such standards will also help to assure that two or more different auditing groups would come up with the same conclusions if they were working with the same source data and using the same guidelines.

It would be desirable for management to develop a set of auditing standards when the system is first installed. Ideally, auditors should be involved from the start—that is, during the preinstallation phase or system design—so as to lay the groundwork for effective controls. Standards may be written up formally or informally agreed upon. The three main sources of standards are:

1. Any suggestions contained in the documentation that shows how the system was designed to work. This source may be adequate if the documentation is complete and up to date.
2. Management mandate. It is possible that auditors will be directed into a particular area, and management may establish a specific minimum or a precise set of criteria to be used as the standard.
3. The auditor's opinion. This is the source that may often prevail, if simply because system documentation is poor and management has not provided any useful criteria.

Note that there are no generally accepted standards for EDP auditing comparable to those governing many other accounting practices, nor do such principles seem to be in sight for data processing auditing in the near future. Furthermore, even if there were some generally acceptable standards, many organizations would not (or may not want to) take advantage of them.

Several auditors have told me how they had been burned on this point. They issued some standards, but operating people unfortunately accepted them as if they were rigid rules that had been cast in concrete. In fact, the standards had been designed by people who had little experience in situations that were rapidly changing. When the auditor wanted to improve on what he had already done, he was told that he had previously issued "instructions" that were now being carefully followed and couldn't be changed easily. Perhaps this type of problem can be overcome by more careful wording of anything that will be treated as a standard.

CONTROLS

The purpose of a control is to make sure a system is working the way it should. Good controls presuppose carefully developed standards that help the EDP department, users, management, and auditors decide when performance is unacceptable, satisfactory, or optimal.

As we collect actual results, we compare them to the relevant standards and calculate a difference, or a variation. Some amount of variation is usually acceptable. When the amount of variation is greater than the limit that was adopted as being acceptable, we have to make a basic decision: Are we going to bring actual results in line with our standards, or are some of the standards unrealistic and perhaps in need of revision?

Even if we performed better than the standard, however, there is a problem. One question that should be asked is: Are we spending too much to get such good results? Perhaps something less would do. Alternatively, we may decide that our standards should be raised.

Internal auditing should have as one of its objectives to help all people in an organization in the effective discharge of their duties. This is partially accomplished by following up on all activities to see if they are properly controlled.

Controls may be classified in a number of ways. One approach is to break them down into preventive, detective, or corrective.

Preventive controls are designed to keep something from happening. For example, a feasibility study should prevent the adoption of a system that doesn't have a good chance of succeeding. Another preventive control is the use of well-designed input forms that minimize recording errors.

No matter how well designed our preventive controls are, some errors will occur, and we need ways to find out about them. This is accomplished by means of *detective controls*. An example of such a control is key verification, a method used to catch keypunching errors. Computer editing is another example; it is designed to catch invalid source data before they can enter the computer.

Finally, despite all our efforts to prevent or detect errors, some will occur and pass all detective controls. Through one of several methods, the error will eventually be recognized. *Corrective controls* are designed as protection against such situations. Examples include the use of backup files to reconstruct data when a file has been destroyed and insurance against loss from a fire.

The distinction between preventive or detective controls is not always clear-cut. For example, does key verification really detect errors in keypunched data or does it prevent errors in source data from getting to the computer? Such fine theoretical points, however, are less important than the use of the proper control for each exposure.

Another way to classify controls is as either positive or negative. For example, in the confirmation of accounts receivable, asking the customer to respond in any event is a positive control; asking for a response only if there is a discrepancy is a negative control.

To take another example, suppose certain data have been converted from the written medium to a computer-readable form by a keypunching process. One way to check if the conversion process was accurate is to key-verify each record; this is a positive control. Another way is to take some relevant total from both the source data and the converted data (whether the latter are on cards, tapes, or discs) and compare the two totals; if they agree, the assumption is that each record has been converted accurately. This is a negative control.

As a final example, suppose an airline has a problem with people showing up with tickets that have been stolen in blank form and then made out by the thief. Management decides to crack down on this by carefully looking at all tickets as they are presented for use. If the numbers of all tickets legally sold by various authorized agents are made available to a computer, then the computer can quickly determine if a ticket presented is valid. This is a positive control. On the other hand, the various ticket sales agencies might report the numbers of only the stolen tickets to the airline computer. Now the system just checks to see if the ticket presented is on the bad list—a negative control. Although the negative method is faster and cheaper, it isn't as sound as the positive control, because there is a good chance that the theft of some tickets went undiscovered.

Generally, a positive control does a better job than a negative control does. On the other hand, negative controls usually cost less to administer. Each control has a specific purpose, works in a particular way, has a specific level of effect, costs a certain amount to put into effect, and has a relative ease of use.

HOW THE EDP AUDITOR PROCEEDS

Selection of Audit Topics

As an auditor proceeds to perform an audit of data processing, he will probably be faced with a major problem in determining exactly what to look at. There are so many areas, each with its widely varying activities, problems, and personalities. Something must be done to help select specific areas for investigation. (Of course, once an EDP operation has been audited, it should become easier to select the topics for future audits.)

The following two methods might be used to make the selection:

1. Determine which of the five key points—accuracy, efficiency, fraud prevention, security, or effectiveness—appear to be most important. It may be possible to collect data showing their relative impacts on net income. Frequently, effectiveness will be investigated anyway, at least to some degree.
2. Carefully review any aspect of operations that tends to erode the customer base. For example, if a poor computerization of a customer billing system causes the business to lose several hundred customers a day, this may be the first area to audit and straighten out. Whereas it may be possible to temporarily live with some inefficiencies or lack of accuracy, erosion of the customer base can hardly be tolerated. It may not take much of a study to determine where the trouble is; the application with the highest costs or the most errors is an obvious candidate.

In addition, there may be a management mandate or a request from users to audit specific areas or aspects of the system. As previously suggested, a user request for an audit indicates that auditing has reached a certain level of maturity. Normally, an audit is the last thing anyone wants.

From management's point of view, since a basic premise of auditing is that any segment of operation is subject to review, the auditor should have a wide degree of latitude in making the choice of what area(s) will be audited.

Defining the Audit Objectives

Once the area to be audited has been selected, the auditor should develop an audit objective, or perhaps several of them. This is necessary to direct or guide the auditor into specific areas. Considering that most audits are of going concerns, it is unlikely that a "100 percent" audit would take place unless the organization was about to be sold or had just discovered that it was the victim of a massive fraud; thus, the objectives of the audit will tend to determine its scope.

Audit objectives will closely relate to the type of auditor

involved, whether that person be an internal or an external auditor or a representative of a government agency. While the external auditor's objectives would most likely involve the financial statements, the internal auditor's objectives might cover data processing in its broadest sense. Furthermore, the internal auditor may do some preparatory work with the objective of reducing the external auditor's fee.

Formulating an Audit Strategy

Having determined the areas and objectives of the audit, the auditor must develop a strategy for implementation. The following general plan may serve as a guideline:

Step 1: Gain an understanding of how the system is supposed to work. Generally, the auditor will not know enough about each segment of the operation to bypass this step. There often will be—and always should be—some documentation that indicates what the system is supposed to do and how. This information may be found, in rather general terms, in minutes of management meetings or memoranda. More specific details are hopefully available from systems analysis documentation such as flowcharts, procedure manuals, and training manuals. One side benefit of regular audits is that auditors' insistence on such essential documentation provides an additional incentive for its creation.

Step 2: Check how the system actually works. This can be accomplished through a combination of observation, interviews, tracing, and cross-checking. Tracing involves following a transaction from inception to completion—for example, to see how the source data on a time card were processed to end up on a paycheck. In cross-checking, the data obtained from one interviewee may be compared to that obtained from another person.

Both auditors and those audited must get reasonably comfortable with the idea that you can trust a person only up to a point—there comes a time when an auditor must double-check with others to make sure that all statements and "facts" tie together as they should. As a result of this step, the auditor may well find that actual operation varies somewhat from the original design as determined in Step 1.

Step 3: Test the system to see what it really produces. This is done by creating sample data and following them to see how well controlled the system is. Perhaps error rates are developed. Costs may be established. This phase also includes such things as confirming balances and observing other processes that will be described later.

Step 4: Evaluate how close the system comes to achieving its original objective. There is no reason why this evaluation can't state that a system is effective when that is the case; apparently, some auditors tend to set overambitious standards in this respect and never say anything good.

In order to evaluate system effectiveness it is necessary to have reasonably clear-cut standards. It is only in this way that one can determine how good or how bad a system is. Even so, it is not easy to evaluate in an entirely objective manner. I compare this situation to the process I use in grading student exams. As I prepare an exam, I make lists of the likely responses and put each one in a category of excellent, good, fair, poor, and so on, using various criteria. Then, when actually evaluating the exams, I put the various answers into those previously established categories. Occasionally, however, I will come across a response that I had not previously thought of. For any answer of that type, I just put each one into the appropriate category as I come to it, taking care to treat all the "new" responses with the same criteria I used in setting up the original standards.

The evaluation phase is obviously a critical one. Great care must be taken to make sure that the lack or obvious failure of a system feature doesn't become the basis of a negative report when in fact there is an adequate compensating control elsewhere. In the interest of establishing an atmosphere of trust and fairness, there should be some commendation when a job is well done; on the other hand, if money is spent on some features of operation that do not produce a reasonable return, this must of course be brought out in the report.

Step 5: Prepare proposals for improvements. It is one thing to criticize something and yet another to be able to recommend needed changes. In fact, management may be wise to adopt an internal standard that all negative auditor criticism be listened to only if accompanied by suggestions for improvement. Evidently, this would make EDP auditing a much more challenging job, and it would call for sound knowledge of computer processes on the part of the auditor.

Auditors may take the opportunity to consider some top-level EDP-related issues at the time they are deciding what is to be their next assignment. For example, it may be worthwhile to review some of the major policies of the organization. Some examples are:

- Is the organization involved in some business that it should abandon? Although this topic may be considered to be the province of the board of directors, most boards can use fresh ideas, suggestions, and perspectives. Internal auditors may be requested to provide such insight.
- Is credit extension to customers too tight or too loose?
- If there is a policy of leasing all major equipment, does this in fact lead to higher costs than obtaining those same items by outright purchase?
- Could EDP provide a major new customer service with great potential? Examples would be: compounding daily interest by a bank on savings accounts; providing much faster claims service at an insurance company; speeding up registration into courses by a college.
- Would the board of directors welcome new thoughts on or a review of the objectives relating to sales growth and profit rates?

Issues such as these have far-reaching implications and demand a creative approach to EDP auditing as well as to internal auditing in general. Any resulting changes may call for substantial changes in the data processing area.

Specific Auditing Techniques

What specific techniques does the auditor use to perform his job? Here are some of the techniques that are commonly employed:

Have people fill out questionnaires.
Obtain, read, and understand documentation.
Interview and question people personally.
Identify, verify, examine, test, trace, reconcile, reperform, and cross-check all activities and records on a sample basis.
Observe operations.

These techniques have always been appropriate to a manual system, and they may be used in a computer system as well. Essentially they involve the testing of controls. Apart from these, there are specialized techniques that are useful only in computerized systems; their use requires that an auditor have some minimal ability to work with and understand computers and/or to direct others so as to provide the desired results. Some of these techniques are:

- Using audit programs. These are programs the auditor uses to run the same data that the client processed. The results of the two executions are compared. The programs themselves are generally obtained commercially; they are written so as to be applicable to a variety of purposes and applications of many users.
- Using test decks. In this situation, the auditor uses data he prepared to run through the client's programs. Since the auditor knows what the computer answers should be, he compares computer results to see how well the program works.
- Checking file dumps. A file dump is simply a printout of the data appearing on magnetic media such as tapes or discs. Although this is a tedious way of checking out de-

tail, it may be required in order to prove the contents of a file.
- Reviewing a client's program logic. This method, once touted as the way of the future, has not become very popular. Another person's logic can become difficult to follow. Even if an auditor can determine that the logic is satisfactory, it still remains to prove that this logic is the one actually used in the computer processing of the job.

SOME AUDITING PITFALLS

Auditors have historically been known for finding faults in the work of those whom they audit; presumably, this is what they are paid for. But being human, auditors have their own faults as well. A survey study of computer center managers brought out the following complaints about those who function as computer auditors:

- There often is too much concern with specific techniques rather than with objectives. Many auditors seem to have pet techniques that they would always like to see in use regardless of the circumstances. Emphasis on objectives would be more desirable because it would lead to a clearer definition of the problem—and a good problem definition usually means you are half way through to a solution.
- Many auditors fail to see the forest for the trees. What is needed is a broad perspective. The main objective of a business is to make money and survive, not to have controls. Controls are tools, not ends in themselves.
- There is widespread failure among auditors to consider the cost-benefit relationship in recommending controls.
- Audits and resulting advice are often late. Not enough essential work is done early enough when a suggestion would have a better chance of being used. (This can be translated into "Get involved at design time.")

These, then, are some observations by data processing specialists about computer auditors. They should be useful to both auditors, who might use such criticism in a constructive sense, and managers, who need to review the work of auditors, develop more effective internal auditors, or select new external or internal auditors.

2

Preinstallation Activities

The time span of preinstallation activities ranges all the way from the point when computerization is first considered until physical installation takes place. This chapter, however, is concerned mainly with the planning and decision making needed to order a computer. The major details of getting ready for installation—namely, designing the various systems and providing the computer programs—are covered in later chapters.

PREINSTALLATION GOALS

The goals of preinstallation activities are relatively few and straightforward. Assuming an organization presently has no computer, a study must be made to determine if it would be worthwhile to get one. Considering how many computer failures there have been, it appears that there have not been enough sound studies of this sort. In many cases the preinstallation study may not be done properly because it is a foregone conclusion that a computer will be ordered.

In determining whether a computer system will be worthwhile, the major tool to use is a cost-benefit analysis. In this context, it is usually best to concentrate on tangible benefits and discount the value of intangible benefits as much as possible. This conservative approach is especially recommended since tangible benefits are usually overstated; if intangible benefits do in fact accrue, they will at least partially offset that potential loss.

To the organization that already has a computer, preinstallation activities comprise evaluation of the current system and comparison with available alternatives. While it is true that the typical organization does not replace its computer(s) as quickly as it did 10 or 15 years ago, the stakes are now no doubt larger than they were before. Therefore, the topic is gaining importance for these organizations. In any event, the typical system is probably geared to cover the next three to five years, so one of the goals of preinstallation activities is to set the direction that will be followed for those future years.

One important issue that must be addressed during the preinstallation phase is the question of which applications the computer should be used for. Other critical aspects are the selection of suitable resources, including hardware facilities and data processing personnel, and determination of the environment—for instance, batch or real time—in which the system is to be used.

THE ROLE OF A STEERING COMMITTEE

It would be extremely unwise to turn all preinstallation activities over to computer specialists or to those who will become employees of the computer center if and when it is established. The recommended approach is to establish a steering committee composed of perhaps five to eight people. There should be a high-ranking member from each major potential user department such as accounting, marketing, or manufacturing. It is usually not feasible to have a member from every department that will be served, because the group would be so large as to be ineffective. If no auditor is actually included in the committee, at least there should be one designated who will promptly review the committee's recommendations.

One of the first roles of the steering committee is to select the people who will make a preliminary survey (see the next section). Once that preliminary survey has been completed, and assuming it provides a positive recommendation to proceed, the steering committee should have the task of deciding who will be permanently assigned to the computer activity. Consider the following situation:

The RST Company has decided to computerize the inventory control function, which up to now has been completely manual. The following candidates have reached the final selection stage:

1. Bill—he has just graduated from college with a degree in computer science, emphasizing mathematical models.
2. Elaine—she has had 25 years of experience with a manual inventory control system at another firm.
3. Hank—he started out at the RST Company in the supply department; he eventually worked his way up to manager of inventory control.
4. Pete—he has been the data processing manager for four companies in the area.

On the basis of these brief data, which person should be chosen? It appears that few people would select Bill. Although he may have a tremendous future with computers, he has had no practical experience with computers, managing, or inventory control. The time required to get a payoff from him may be too long.

Among the other three candidates, my choice would be Hank. He has experience in the functional area (inventory control), and he knows the company and its politics. He can learn what he needs to know about computers easier than Pete can learn about both inventory control and the RST Company. Also, Hank can learn what he needs to know quicker than

Elaine could become familiar with both computers and the RST Company.

As organizations gain more experience with computerized applications, they realize that the manager of the computer center must be more of a manager than a technician. That factor would cause many current selection processes to favor Hank.

The future well-being of the whole organization is resting heavily on such personnel decisions. Who is better qualified than key managers to make the decisions involving the initial selection of people?

At the point where it is necessary to make critical decisions about computerization, many organizations that do not have computers feel they don't have the necessary qualifications in-house to make much of a feasibility study. Thus they call in a consultant or perhaps even use the services of a computer manufacturer. It is my personal opinion that at this point the major issues relate to internal systems, personalities, and politics rather than to computer details. My own advice is to spend the money necessary to teach the appropriate employees what they need to know about computers. Perhaps the feasibility study will be somewhat slowed, but the results should be more relevant than otherwise. This is not to suggest that consultants should not be used. They can be used to give ideas and direction, but employees of the organization should do most of the work.

Once the preinstallation activities are completed, some organizations prefer to disband the steering committee. But there is some merit in continuing it, especially from the standpoint of its setting priorities as to the applications that are to be computerized. There is a danger of paying the most attention to the potential user who makes the greatest noise; the use of the committee can provide some objectivity otherwise not available. Consider the following situation:

The management of ABC Company is trying to determine which computer applications need redesign and the order in which such redesign should be done. The following applications are the main candidates:

Application	Problem
1. Customer Invoicing	Invoices always seem to be about five days late going out.
2. Payroll	It costs about 39 cents to prepare a payroll check. Competitors say their unit cost is 33 cents.
3. Quality Control	Four percent of shipments to customers are returned defective. Warranty costs are up 7 percent.
4. Shipping	It requires about eight days after receipt of an order to ship most off-the-shelf items.

This is an ideal situation for a steering committee to get involved in. ABC Company needs the broad perspective that can be obtained only by getting input from all the major functional areas. An undesirable approach would be to think of using the computer only to cut costs, in which case payroll would most likely be selected first. A more objective approach would be to determine, for each of the four areas, the negative impact noncomputerization would have on the future of the business. A well-thought-out analysis would probably suggest that the customer base needs help more than payroll costs. Thus quality control and shipping might be selected first. In fact, they may give the payroll system a low priority for an indefinite period.

Some organizations have chosen not to use the steering committee approach. Others have given it lip service only, allowing designated members never to attend or to send lower-level employees as delegates. What reasons could management conceivably have for not getting properly involved, other than the excuse that there is not enough time? Some reasons commonly advanced are:

The topic is too technical. The equipment is complicated, the people are technical specialists, and the field is full of jargon. These arguments simply don't hold. It is surprising how much one can learn about computers in just a few hours, provided proper training methods are used. It might be well to assign the responsibility for reviewing the quality of internal training programs to a competent internal auditor.

We have already hired the best technicians we can get. That could be the very problem, especially if there is some assumption that technicians will make good managers. The major problems are usually management and people problems, not technical problems. You can't afford to let the technicians make the decisions that should be left up to professional managers.

All you need to do is. . . . The salesman said so. Unfortunately, sales representatives may not disclose, or even know, all the potential problems of the proposed computer or system.

So-and-so is close to retirement and is not about to learn anything new. If this is a prevailing attitude, then management must decide how much it will allow it to impede the progress of the organization.

THE PRELIMINARY SURVEY

The objective of a preliminary survey is to determine if it is worthwhile to proceed to a more extensive feasibility study (discussed in the next section). There are a number of legitimate reasons for getting a computer; there is no point in making up an excuse for doing so. Within an organization there probably is already a body of knowledge, though perhaps rather informal, about problems with some of the present systems. Such items as excessive or rapidly rising personnel costs, excessive errors, timing problems, competitive situations, or a desire to do something not practical with a manual system would be key reasons for considering a computer system. Hopefully the "ego factor" is no longer present or can be discovered if it is.

The key elements to concentrate on are what a computer can and can't do and whether the organization has the kind of people who can and will adjust to the discipline required by a computer. A computer can read data from several sources, such as cards, tape, or discs; it can perform all forms of arithmetic well; and it can display its answers in many forms (cards, tape, disc, printed on paper, and so on). Furthermore, it can perform arithmetic subject to specific conditions, such as deducting Social Security tax from gross pay only until the cutoff point has been reached, provided such conditions have been properly integrated into a computer program. Also, the computer can readily store data for later use.

On the other hand, the computer can do only what it is programmed to do. If a required step is missing, the computer just can't provide for that step. The computer has no judgment; thus it would subtract overtime pay from regular pay if programmed to do so. Some organizations just aren't cut out to use computers effectively because of the people they have. For example, computer systems have been installed in many situations where management thought the computer would alleviate the problems caused by slow, error-prone, and incompetent personnel. If that's the kind of staff you are going to have to work with, the computer isn't going to work well. Successful use of a computer requires good, competent people.

In one company, a quick feasibility study by a consultant was the basis for placing an order for a computer. Although the justification to the management committee was sketchy and certainly wouldn't have passed if the request had been for any other investment, no one questioned it. Thus the computer was ordered, and systems development and computer programming began.

However, it soon became obvious that several existing employees in mechanical data processing operations were not cut out to be computer specialists. Nonetheless, they were allowed to be part of the new team, but their intended roles were not made clear. Furthermore, no manager had ever been appointed for the group. It was top management's view that it would soon be obvious to everyone who the most knowledgeable person was. Workers would slowly begin to respect that person as being the boss, but no one's feelings would be hurt early in the project because of any announcement. Management predicted it could safely make such an announcement within a year.

But without a clear indication as to who was the boss and with even less of a plan, the people were not working on the items that should have had the highest priorities. Much attention was given to certain technical details, but one of the most important items was almost totally overlooked—the raw data input and its format had still not been pinned down within 60 days of the scheduled installation.

As the problems mounted, the president at last called in the internal auditor to study the situation. The auditor's first effort was to study the economic justification. He found that a part of the justification had used one of the oldest ploys around: letting the computer installation take credit for some savings to which it had no direct relationship. The major application involved the inventory control system, and the original study showed that enough clerical people would be released to more than pay for the computer and still leave a handsome profit. That meant the study did not even have to rely upon any intangible savings that might be generated by such things as faster reports and better service.

The existing inventory control system worked roughly as follows. When a customer order was received, it was sent immediately to inventory control posting clerks, who proceeded to reserve the requested quantity of products for that customer. Then the order flowed back through the credit department for a financial check and to the order entry department to have shipping documents prepared. The shipping documents went to the warehouse, where the product was released for shipment to the customer. Then shipping information was sent to inventory control, where the "reservation" was canceled and the amount shipped was deducted from the perpetual on-hand amount.

At about the same time that the computer study was being undertaken by one group, another group was studying the inventory control system per se, because some people in the firm had an instinctive feeling there was too much paperwork involved in inventory control. The reason for the double-pass against inventory records was looked into. It was found that it related back to World War II, when the company had adopted the "reservation" idea because of war-time shortages and the need to allocate inventory carefully. It was quickly concluded that the reservation feature of the system had long since lost its usefulness and should be eliminated. Thus a major mistake made on the computer system justification was that it compared the costs and benefits of the computer approach not to the best manual approach available, but to an obsolete and inefficient manual system.

When these findings were reported to the president, he asked for a complete investigation of the computer situation. The internal auditor therefore made a full study and reported the following:

1. The computer group did not have a recognized leader. Thus it was floundering about without any direction.
2. No schedule had ever been prepared as to what should be accomplished by whom at what time.
3. A person "donated" by the computer manufacturer was being used at the detail level of writing programs instead of at a much broader, desired level of instruction, problem definition, and setting standards.
4. Certain inventory control functions were being computerized even though users of the system did not want those features regardless of how they would be provided.
5. Systems analysts were not being treated as a cost of the proposed computer operation. Their salaries were deemed to be a fixed cost of the company, whether or not a computer was obtained.
6. Although computerization of the inventory control system would eliminate some existing manual functions at each of 25 regional warehouses, the computer justification study, by assuming elimination of 13 full-time people, had taken too much credit in this area.

Faced with such overwhelming evidence that showed the proposed computer system would represent an out-of-pocket cost of several hundred thousand dollars instead of a saving of a like amount, the project was canceled. By the time that cancellation occurred, however, a great deal of money had already been spent, and several people had been either hired or moved from other positions in the company to work in the computer department. Much of that effort and most of the resulting hard feelings could have been avoided if a proper audit had been made at the proper time.

If the need for a computer is really there, and if installation of a computer system is feasible from a personnel point of view, the next step is to determine what a computerized system would cost.

The cost of the computer itself can be roughly estimated by making informal inquiries at computer vendors and getting in touch with other organizations that have installed comparable systems in the recent past. A rule of thumb can be used to estimate the total system cost. For example, total system cost currently is roughly three times the basic hardware cost.

Through this process, hopefully a solid go/no-go decision can be made before a great deal of money is spent.

THE FEASIBILITY STUDY

A feasibility study will be performed only if the preliminary survey results in a positive recommendation. Because of its much more detailed nature, a feasibility study will take significantly more time.

At this point several applications may be studied in some depth, though there is often one major application that will be the impetus for considering a computer. Examples of such major applications are combined systems for order entry/inventory control/billing/accounts receivable, production scheduling/manufacturing/quality control, or purchasing/accounts payable. Single applications such as payroll or billing are unlikely candidates since they are normally not extensive enough to consume a major portion of computer time. It is the combination of several subsystems into a logical unit that produces the major candidates.

In any event, it is essential to clearly define the problem that is to be solved. Generally, a good problem definition will take you 50 to 75 percent of the way toward problem solution.

PREINSTALLATION ACTIVITIES   43

Consider the following example. I came across a company that received 50 percent of all its sales orders from the field in the last three working days of the month. This obviously strained many departments at month end, besides leaving them with idle capacity much of the rest of the month.

Company officials jumped to the conclusion that the solution to the problem was to computerize order entry and related systems. The mistake they made was that they did not define the problem that caused the uneven workload; they were ready to accept the lopsided volume as a fact of life and just find a way of handling it.

When the company looked more closely at the issue, they realized the reason for the month-end rush of sales orders was that each company salesperson had a maximum pay that he or she could earn. Because of this, salespeople withheld customer orders until month end and submitted only those required to bring them up to their maximum. Surplus orders were submitted in the following month, and if necessary, sales representatives would take several days off work to make sure they didn't produce results for which there was no pay.

My recommendation was to remove all upper pay limits for sales representatives. But that was quickly rejected, largely because the egos of several officers would have been badly bruised if a salesperson would have earned more than they. The solution eventually adopted was to settle sales commissions every six months instead of every month. At least this created the order-processing bottleneck only twice a year instead of twelve times a year.

Much of a feasibility study will be concerned with how systems work, the anticipated volumes of transactions, and changes that would be desirable. A good feasibility study should uncover enough items that, if changed, would create a benefit that will pay for the cost of the study even if computerization is not followed. A common example is the elimination of duplicate reports.

Certain efforts will be made to show how the system could work using the computer. Perhaps analysts will go so far as to computerize sample data from one application and obtain a program to process these data on a computer. This is done so that times and capacities can be estimated well enough to elevate computer vendors' proposals. Obviously, one should expect every vendor to submit a proposal indicating that his firm's computer can do the job well.

A key point in conducting a feasibility study is to search carefully for potential trouble spots, pitfalls, and limitations. It is this practice that, if properly carried out, may result in a recommendation to stay away from computerization. This will avoid being in a position where you have a system you don't like but stick with it because no one wants to walk away from an investment that has already been made. For example, if lack of money is the real reason for a company's chronic inventory shortages, computerization of inventory control will not solve that problem. Perhaps computerization of accounts receivable and tighter policies on the granting of credit are areas that should be addressed. Also, departments in which procedures are constantly changing because of personnel turnover might not be compatible with the more disciplined approach required for effective computer use.

One sound way to get help here is to talk to others who have already been through this experience. (But be sure to deal with people whom you can trust.) Find out what kinds of problems they have, and ask yourself if your own organization is in a position to deal with these or similar problems.

Another major consideration, of course, is cost. Considerable money must be spent on a computer system for some time before there will be any return. It could take several years before positive results start to show and several more to get the investment back. Also, there are systems analysis, programming, conversion, and parallel-run costs that will be incurred over and above the costs of hardware. When you also consider that most computers don't save money and that many are marginally successful in producing significantly better results, you could be chasing recovery dollars that aren't there. Some organizations literally can't afford the "savings" promised by computerization.

Equipment additions and replacements are typically motivated by deficiencies of the current configuration. But a careful analysis is required to identify inadequate components and avoid enhancing the wrong one or replacing the whole when only a partial change is needed.

The typical business computer run is input/output bound or limited. This means the time it takes to do the whole job is slowed down by input and/or output devices. Most input/output operations are basically mechanical, and hence slow, whereas internal processing is electronic, and hence fast. The crucial point is that the speed of an entire operation is determined by its slowest component.

So what should be done when there are a lot of jobs that are input/output bound? Certainly the last thing to do is to get a new computer that has a faster central processing unit (CPU), because the CPU in the existing computer isn't being used to capacity. You would be better advised to look at your input/output devices. Perhaps there are some faster ones available.

Even if there are faster input/output devices available, however, you may not necessarily want to get them. Examine your various input/output steps. Is every one of them really necessary, or can some of them be eliminated or streamlined? Do you really need all the information currently generated by the system? If it should turn out that there are only a few input/output bound jobs, it may not be practical to change equipment.

Another potential solution to the problem is the use of multiprogramming, which involves running two or more programs at a time. Although this does not cause any individual program to run faster, more programs can be run per time unit, so you get more value out of the expensive CPU.

A feasibility study should include a serious examination of all viable alternatives. There are usually several basically different approaches to each problem solution and many different hardware configurations that could be used. In addition, the possibility of buying computer power from a service center should be considered, since in today's market an organization does not need to have its own computer in order to take advantage of modern data processing techniques.

DOCUMENTATION

For the purpose of preinstallation activities, the documentation file should contain records of everything that happened. This would include copies of any memoranda (especially those from top management establishing the charge of each study group); accurate minutes of meetings; results of any studies regarding computerization; requests for proposals submitted to computer vendors; proposals received from vendors; and the goals and standards established by or agreed to by management.

Such documentation is prepared and retained not just to have a copy for the file, but for later use. Certainly an auditor will need a starting place, and the documented history is a good one. Members of the steering committee and the feasibility study team will occasionally need to refresh their memories on key points. New employees will have to learn what happened. A well-documented file also eliminates unnecessary reperformance of certain steps, such as recounting numbers of transactions or personnel. Finally, documentation establishes a method of determining accountability and measuring performance against initial commitments.

It is desirable that simple documentation standards be established and enforced. In its simplest form, this may call for keeping a daily diary of what each person did on the project. It would be desirable for the manager to review these data each week and summarize them in a meaningful way. In this way, the analysts could provide necessary information in a free-style format without having to create new data-collection forms. Allowing the use of handwritten data may ease some of the burden because it eliminates the hassle that might occur in getting the data typed.

STANDARDS

If preinstallation activities are going to be audited—and they should be before any major commitments are made—then auditors must know what their point of reference is. In other words, there must be some standards against which they can compare what the organization is, or has been, doing.

It is advisable for the organization to establish some formal methods for developing the standards. Certainly top management should lead the way on developing the standards. Also, the people who will have to make the system work—that is, the various employees of the user departments and the data processing specialists—should be involved in setting the standards. It is not absolutely necessary that auditors be present in setting preinstallation standards, although they can participate if that extra element of independence is required.

Standards must be tailor-made for each installation and take account of specific characteristics and requirements. Thus what I offer in this section are examples and not suggestions that are generally valid for any organization. Furthermore, standards are not to be followed slavishly when common sense dictates otherwise. Lastly, the list of standards offered here is not meant to cover all relevant areas.

With these reservations, then, here are some examples of standards for preinstallation activities:

1. The money spent on a computer installation should have a financial payback within three years.
2. The expenditure is to return the same minimum of 15 percent before taxes that is expected of all capital expenditures within the company.
3. Any equipment is to be leased rather than purchased except under the following conditions:
   - When there is a reasonable expectancy that the equipment will be retained longer than six years.
   - When the retention period is expected to be from three to six years, but the cost of buying is not more than 20 percent greater than the cost of leasing, exclusive of equity value at the time of equipment disposal.
4. Under no circumstances will any equipment vendor's standard contract be acceptable to us. The vendor must be willing to negotiate a reasonable number of provisions according to our wishes. Specific areas to be covered include

adequate test facilities at vendor expense prior to installation, vendor guaranty of any programs provided, and conditions under which the contract may be canceled at user option.
5. If a computer center is established, no employee from any other department within the company will be considered for transfer unless he or she has consistently had at least a 75 rating on the Standard Employee Rating Scale Plan. [The computer center can't afford to take on employees that other departments want to get rid of or who can't perform reasonably well wherever they are now.]
6. Major equipment replacements will not be made unless the existing equipment has been operating for at least two years. [But please remember our earlier comment that standards are not rules designed to strangle the organization.]
7. A maximum of three vendors will be in the final running for equipment selection.
8. A multivendor approach is to be reasonably considered. For example, the CPU may be obtained from vendor A, tape and disc drives from vendor B, and the printer from vendor C. This is a practice which has been around long enough that it is known to be workable.
9. If the decision has been made to lease equipment, then third-party leasing arrangements must be considered.
10. No weight will be given to single success reports about any aspect of operation in another organization. There are too many differences among organizations to think that we could be successful with something if we can find only one other place where it has worked well.
11. We will not be a pioneer in the use of any new technique or new piece of equipment.
12. Approximately three-fourths of the feasibility study should be completed before any consideration is given to a specific brand of equipment. [This item is not relevant for those who have previously decided they are going to deal with a specific vendor all the way.]
13. All work is expected to be performed using the rules of common sense and reasonable objectivity.

While there are some problems involved with establishing and using standards, the consequences of proceeding without standards are much more severe. A rather critical report about the lack of standards was issued by the General Accounting Office of the United States in 1978. Although this report was based on the practices of various government agencies only, its conclusions are of general interest. Two of the pitfalls pointed out were:

1. Because nonstandard programming languages are being used, hundreds of millions of dollars are spent annually to convert programs so they can run on the new machines that are obtained. The new computers use a nonstandard language as well, and all the current programs will need to be rewritten again the next time equipment is replaced.

2. Hundreds of millions of dollars are wasted because of the lack of standards in selecting hardware. Suppose an agency insists on using a 78-column punched card instead of the standard 80-column card. If there is only one 78-column-card manufacturer, then the agency is at the mercy of that manufacturer when buying both the card-handling equipment and the cards themselves. The report further stated that the major cause of operating without standards was that the agencies relied too much on industry to develop the standards. GAO suggested that rather than wait, the agencies should take the initiative in setting some standards themselves. When the agencies contended that they did not have the budgets needed to do the necessary work, GAO pointed out that the agencies had not requested any form of help.

It is quite likely that the typical company does not know how much its lack of standards is costing it. Data processing specialists may not wish to volunteer much information about the subject, and they can easily cover up the situation if management hasn't learned enough about computer operations. Such cost information can be obtained by one of two methods: (1) by performing an audit with that specific objective, and (2) by collecting data processing costs in specific categories. What is needed is a breakdown of major cost segments. For example, instead of collecting general programming costs, it is possible to break down the various programming costs according to what caused them. Relevant breakdowns are by user request, changes in the contract with the labor union, and government regulation.

Of course, use of no standards may reflect a temporary situation. Each situation must be carefully evaluated on its own merits. In many cases a new manager may have inherited some undesirable practices in a department, and it may take a while to replace them with desirable practices.

CONTROLS

Until now in this chapter, we were concerned with what should be done prior to the installation of a computer, whether we are dealing with a first-time installation, the replacement of an existing computer, or a contracted computer service. Now we are concerned with the kinds of things that should be done to make sure the organization is getting the best possible chance to obtain an effective computer system (if indeed it needs a computer system at all). The auditor should look at all the foregoing steps and the related controls to be discussed.

The major control in preinstallation activities involves the effective use of the steering committee. It is the job of that committee to make sure that basic, reasonable procedures are followed, just as they would be in any other endeavor. The committee should either directly or by delegation attend to the following points:

1. Ensure that top management periodically confirms existing policies or sees that new or changed policies are promptly communicated to all concerned. The need for such prompt, timely action is illustrated by the cartoon in Figure 4.
2. Make careful and timely reviews of any time and cost budgets that were developed and/or used in the preinstallation activities.
3. Make a critical analysis of any reports that show that a new system will result in an immediate reduction in processing costs, since this rarely happens.
4. If there is to be no change in the steps in the system or in the results produced—that is, if existing steps will continue to be performed, only now by a different

Figure 4. The result of poor internal communication. (Reprinted from *Business Automation*, (now *Infosystems*), February 1971, with permission.

machine—question why this should be so. If things are done the right way, the overall system should probably exhibit major changes, both in its logic and in its results.

5. Insist upon an actual computer run of the company's own data (for a significant application) from any computer vendor making a bid. This may help identify problems beforehand.

6. Solicit pertinent comments from several potential internal users as to how they view the practicality of computerization. If a new system is installed either without input from users or over their protests, it will never work well.

7. Require that a substantial list of disadvantages accompany every proposal submitted by either internal analysts or vendors. It is unrealistic that a proposal would have only good features to offer.

An effective way for the steering committee to make sure it is doing everything it should is to use checklists. These are often supplied by computer vendors, CPA firms, and consultants. Also friends in other organizations should be able to supply a lot of valuable ideas.

Of course the group or person to whom the steering committee reports should periodically review its work to determine if the committee is functioning as it should. Such review could reside with the board of directors, the president, or a top-ranking manager.

CONCERNS WITH NEW METHODS

The field of data processing is constantly developing new equipment and new ways of doing things. This creates not only new opportunities, but also new challenges and problems. This section covers two recent developments, namely, the large-scale use of minicomputers and of "data bases."

Minicomputers

For many years, most of the computers on the market were relatively large machines that were used in a centralized fashion. Usually, the computer was physically placed at the home office of the organization. Raw data were sent by all the source areas to the computer center, where they were processed, and the results were returned to the users. The computer center had a staff of data entry people (keypunching and verifying), programmers and systems analysts, and computer operators.

Much of this operating philosophy was due to the high fixed cost of operation and the apparent need for specialists to perform computer-related work. Under these circumstances, centralization obviously was the appropriate mode of operation.

One consequence of this was some user dissatisfaction. Communication with computer specialists tended to be poor because of their professional jargon, and they were often hard to deal with. Sometimes they worked on what they wanted to rather than on user priorities. Implementation was often much

behind schedule, and needed changes were difficult to make after installation.
Now the minicomputer has entered the picture. Physically smaller than its predecessor, and cheaper, it nonetheless offers a surprising amount of power. To make the acquisition of a minicomputer attractive to a user, most vendors offer a package of programs that are presumably all ready to go. The theory is instant computing—the ability of a department, formerly depending totally upon a centralized data processing department, to do its own thing. If the user still has a relationship with the main computer center as far as sending data to the central computer for consolidation into the organization's overall system, this concept of operation is often referred to as *distributed processing*.

Not long ago it was a rule of thumb that centralization was the way to go because it was cheaper. This was the case because a large computer was deemed to be much more efficient than a number of smaller computers. Now some of the people who previously "proved" that brand of economics are "proving" that it is cheaper to distribute processing power. It will take a concerted effort by management and auditors to look carefully at all proposals that seek to justify the use of distributed processing on the basis of dollar savings.

If the relevant issue in centralized processing is incompetency on the part of computer specialists or the inability of the organization to find enough good people to get all the needed work finished in reasonable time, then management will expect some strong assurance that a new processing method will overcome such deficiencies. We have to make sure we don't end up with distributed incompetence.

Data Base Management

Historically, each application in an organization was an entity unto itself, and each had its own set of files. However, many applications had data that overlapped with others. For example, cost data may have existed in budgets, purchasing, accounts payable, and cost accounting. This not only expanded the total size of all the files because of the duplication but also created extra work needed to coordinate the efforts of file maintenance.

The data base concept helps alleviate those problems. Under a data base system, a unit of data is stored in only one place. The data base system, a set of complex programs, keeps track of that location, and as any application is being run, the need for any unit of data is determined and the computer obtains it from wherever it is stored.

Unfortunately, the use of a data base creates its own problems. When each application had its own distinct set of files, the problem of data security was not so far-reaching. Each file could be protected on a basis appropriate to its own specific problems. A user could even conveniently provide a means of file backup. Similarly, preventing unauthorized access to files is less difficult under a traditional system than with a data base. Finally, the problems that an auditor has in pulling data from a file for audit purposes can be compounded.

When computer specialists are proposing something like a data base management system, auditors should be involved in the decision as to whether to adopt it or not. If auditors are not at all competent in this area but reject any proposals with the excuse that the proposed system is not auditable, then management must determine which side is taking the more objective position. It might be well for management to have a brief seminar on the topic to help make that determination.

AUDITING PREINSTALLATION ACTIVITIES

While it is common for an auditor to come in after the system is fully installed and to point out errors and deficiencies, it is far better to be involved from the beginning and to help to prevent incorrect steps from being taken.

As discussed in Chapter 1, there are a number of methods at the auditor's disposal, including the use of questionnaires, checking the documentation, interviewing people, testing transactions, and observing operations. The auditor will be selecting those procedures which will determine whether preinstallation activities were reasonably performed and controlled. The remainder of this chapter will give details about auditing specifically for accuracy, efficiency, fraud, security, and effectiveness.

Accuracy

Feasibility studies have a way of using inaccurate methods that tend to result in overoptimistic predictions of savings. The major error is underestimating the resources that will be needed, particularly time requirements, both for people and equipment. By the time the error is discovered, the system is usually well underway. At that time it is considered too late to turn back, so the authorization is obtained to increase resources, at whatever additional cost, and the projected savings are correspondingly reduced or may even evaporate into a loss.

The most common preinstallation errors responsible for such inaccurate estimates are:

1. Using too high a figure in terms of productive hours per day. If working hours are, say, from 8 A.M. to 5 P.M., with an hour for lunch, there is a tendency to project on the basis of eight productive hours per day. When you consider the usual coffee break each morning and each afternoon, other times spent for personal reasons, and the customary time needed for getting started and getting stopped, six hours may be a more realistic figure to use.

There should be some realistic data within the organization as to what this number actually is, and that figure should be used. (Perhaps there is a place here for a standard to be applied.) In any event, it is unlikely that a new system per se will increase the number of productive hours per day unless a significant management action causes the amount to improve.

2. Using averages in an unrealistic manner. Suppose a company has calculated that there are an average of 1,000 transactions a day. Assuming that in a six-hour day (see point 1 above) a person can process 200 transactions, the conclusion may be reached that five people are needed to handle all transactions. The problem is that there is no average day; transactions tend to occur haphazardly. They usually bunch up near the end of

Figure 5. Examples of system flowcharts with inadequate treatment of error correction.

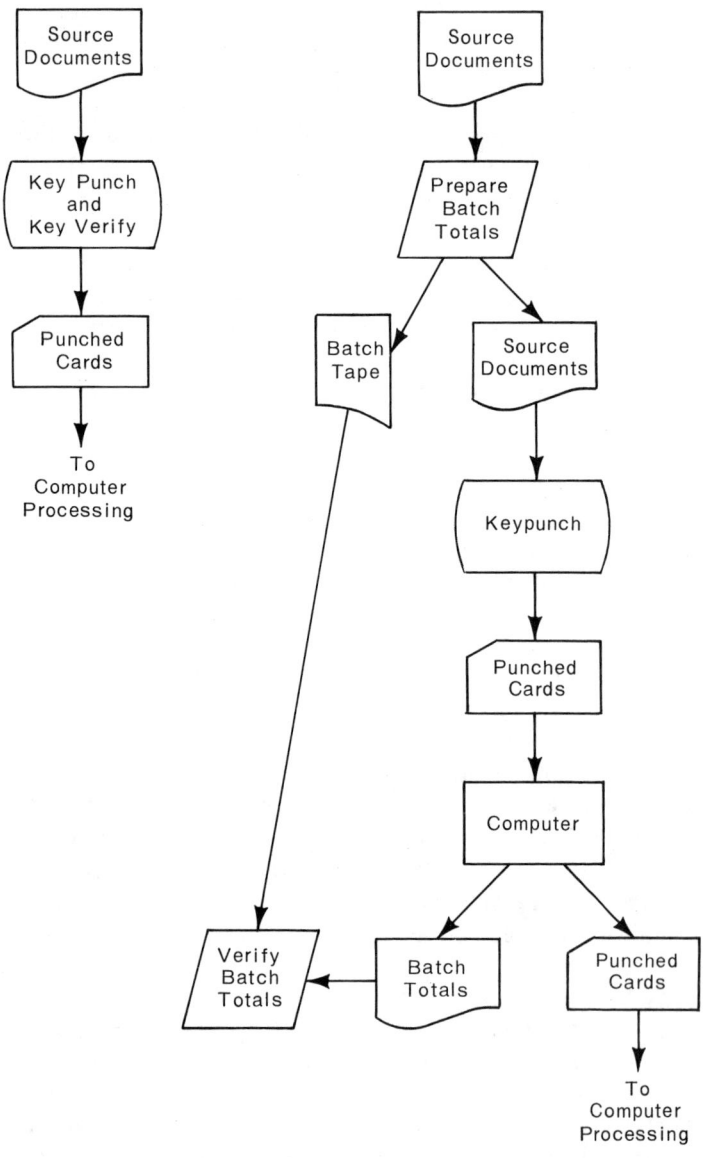

the week and also at the end of the month. Since most organizations want current data or reports (this may, after all, have been the reason to install the system in the first place), processing must be prompt even at such peak-load times. Thus we may need seven or eight people at some times and end up with excess personnel for much of the rest of the time.

One way to solve this problem is to move people around among several jobs; however, in many situations this proves impractical. Another possibility that deserves serious consideration is the use of part-time employees.

3. Improperly attributing a saving to the reduction of activities involving fractional people. Unfortunately, unrelated fractional people do not add up to whole people who can be dismissed.

4. Underestimating time requirements because of the improper use of machine-rated speeds. Machine-rated speeds define how fast a machine can operate if all conditions are ideal. Even though a computer printer can perhaps print 1,000 lines a minute, it most likely won't do that on a production run for a variety of reasons.

5. Failing to properly account for the time needed to handle all the things that go wrong—and there are generally plenty. For example, systems flowcharts often hint at error conditions but do not provide one bit of time to take care of the errors. Figure 5 shows two such flowcharts. In both cases we know there will be some errors (as implied by the word "verify"), but there is no provision for the steps that will correct them and thus no time allotted to correction procedures. More logical ways of designing the steps are shown in the flowcharts in Figure 6, which incorporate explicit error detection and correction steps.

Efficiency

Those who perform preinstallation activities are rarely accused of taking too much time for their task. In fact, the opposite is generally the case. Too little time is spent, and along with that, too little money is invested. Spending more time here and thus doing a thorough job generally pays off later by

Figure 6(a). System flowchart allowing for error correction using key verification.

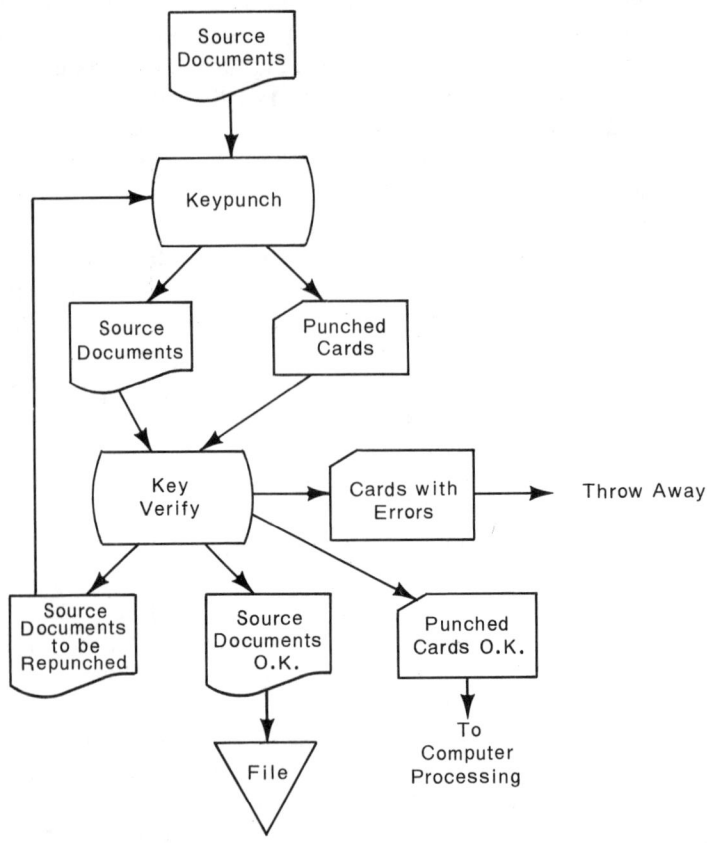

saving time, avoiding trouble spots, or producing quicker or higher-quality results.

The experienced auditor will therefore make sure that plenty of time and a reasonable expense are allotted to preinstallation activities. By the same token, the auditor will question any study that is completed considerably under budget in either regard, because that suggests that an inadequate job may have been done.

A key issue in the efficiency area is that of *leasing* versus

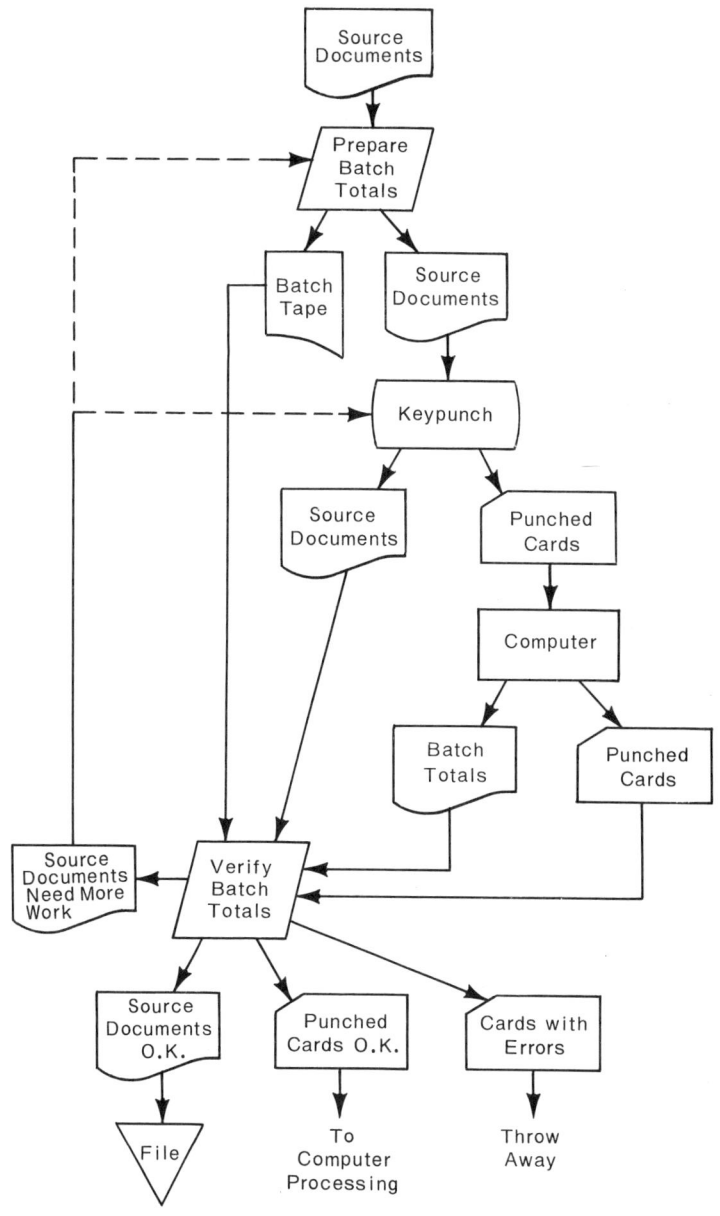

Figure 6(b). System flowchart allowing for error correction using batch totals.

buying.* It is difficult to get accurate information on the dollar split between leasing and buying. Various studies seem to show that leasing accounts for about 75 percent of the acquisitions of the larger machines, whereas minicomputers are more likely to be bought than leased. Some manufacturers have established marketing policies that push the customer in the direction of buying. Our concern here is obviously with those situations where there is a realistic option to go in either direction. (Even if the computer manufacturer does not lease directly to a user, perhaps a deal can be made with a third-party lessor.)

Most likely the major reason given for leasing (from a user's standpoint) is that you can get out of the lease when you want to. Of course, that ability depends on the length of the lease, which is probably for at least a year and possibly much longer. (It appears that the typical lease life may be increasing.) The two main reasons for wanting to get out of a lease are either that you don't need a computer anymore (which is not so likely to happen) or that you don't want to be stuck with an obsolete system.

The idea of a computer being made obsolete by a new one has to be put in its proper perspective. Clearly, the new computer doesn't make the existing one any less able to do the job; it merely means the existing one may not be able to do the job as well as the new one might. Even if you could get rid of the old one and replace it with a new model, that may not be desirable because of certain costs that will be incurred and the disruption in operating the various systems. That one-time cost of conversion must be carefully weighed against possible reductions in annual operating costs with a new computer.

One data center manager I knew had leased some keypunch machines for 18 years. In that time he had effectively paid for them more than three times over. When I asked him why he had leased them for so long, he said he was concerned that new

---

* Although there are technical differences between renting and leasing, for the purpose of this book I will treat both under the heading of leasing, which is used to mean an acquisition method whereby the user is not building up any equity in or right to the asset in question.

machines might come out and obsolete his; leasing, he felt, gave him some protection against this since the machines weren't owned. Although he did not say so, there may have been an additional reason for his decision to lease rather than buy these machines. Internal procedures usually make it much easier to lease. There is less paperwork involved, and you don't have to get as many approvals to make the commitment. This may well be the reason behind many decisions to opt for a lease arrangement.

I personally took advantage of a situation like this once myself when I was a data processing manager. There was a piece of additional equipment I wanted. The vendor salesman was very cooperative. All he needed was a letter from me requesting the item. I wrote the letter, the item was delivered, and the accounting department paid the higher bill. Since our operations were never audited by anyone, there was no need to justify such requests. There were no ripples caused by my action. Although I wasn't considered to be an executive, there was no reason for the salesman to question my authority.

Perhaps the best approach is to remove the lease-or-purchase decision from the data processing manager. Presumably the difference between the costs of leasing and purchasing shouldn't be so great as to have any bearing on whether or not a system will be installed. But it is possible in some cases that a computer would never have been obtained if it couldn't have been accomplished by lease. If the cost difference is so great that you can justify its acquisition by lease but not by purchase, then the whole venture is probably on shaky ground.

Apparently, the leasing option is often chosen because of the impact buying would have on the company's balance sheet. Presumably there is no impact in a lease situation, as none of the important financial ratios gets upset. By contrast, if you buy, you disrupt either current ratios if you pay now with available cash, or debt/equity ratios if you borrow the money. Although the results you report to the world are certainly important, you want to be careful that the nicer-looking presentation made possible by leasing doesn't cost a lot more in total dollars over the long run than the buying method, which does have the effect of making the financial condition look less desirable.

There is another issue here. Some might say that a potential computer user can afford to lease even if he doesn't have the financial capacity to buy. That is a questionable statement. If a company's financial status is so questionable that it is turned down in several attempts to obtain financing to buy, then perhaps it should, at least for the time being, concentrate on some aspect of the business other than getting a computer. It is worthwhile, however, to spend some effort on obtaining computer services through a service bureau arrangement for those applications that really need computerization.

In the final analysis, it is the auditor's task to determine that the major criteria used were endorsed by top management and not motivated by personal feelings or preferences of financial or computer specialists. In this connection, a point made earlier in Chapter 1 is relevant, namely, that auditors can make great contributions by getting top management to review its own policies, goals, and operating methods.

Fraud

The topic of fraud is usually associated less with preinstallation activities than with the day-to-day operation of a system. If you will temporarily accept a somewhat loose definition of fraud, however, it can be shown to be something to be concerned about even at this stage. I will define fraud in this context to include any deliberate attempt to obtain a decision that is harmful to the organization.

Consider the following example. I was once invited to attend, though not to participate in, a presentation to top management. The topic was the justification for getting a computer. Much of the feasibility team's sales pitch dealt with a projected payback in three years. The top managers present were particularly impressed by this, because in other areas they were generally used to paybacks of five to ten years or more. The proposal was accepted without reservation. As everybody left the presentation room, I privately asked the manager of the feasibility team how long they planned to keep the computer; he said two years. Apparently the members of the study team wanted the computer so badly that they were willing to use tactics of that kind to get it. I believe this example meets my criteria above for an act of fraud.

Other situations that can compare to this are where it is obvious that equipment will be obtained from only one certain vendor despite any facts to the contrary (though this could be a company policy) and where obviously incompetent or biased people are used to make the study.

An auditor will have to be lucky to stumble across situations such as those described here. Certainly he would need a relatively free rein to investigate all the areas necessary to dig out such situations. Also, how to go about reporting such practices is a delicate issue.

Security

The major security issue in preinstallation activities involves preventing such things as cost data or new system methods from reaching outsiders, particularly competitors. Auditing will therefore involve checking operating practices to make sure that reasonable caution is taken when sending any information to the outside, requesting information from others, or disclosing plans to various vendors, and generally that reasonable secrecy is maintained for all documentation within the organization. A big part of the job is to stress the need for secrecy, to issue some basic policies on security, and then periodically to follow up on these policies. The most effective control, however, is the methods used to select the individuals who will be performing the various EDP functions.

Effectiveness

Quite often the effectiveness of one step cannot be adequately measured until the results of the next step (or steps) are available. Thus you perhaps can't adequately judge the true effectiveness of preinstallation activities until a year or two after the computer is installed. But most organizations can't wait that long to draw some conclusion about that first effort, and thus something has to be done before management commits itself to go on to the next phase.

Checking for effectiveness involves a review of the original goals and the standards that were adopted. Also, the auditor will have to pay close attention to the issues of accuracy, efficiency, fraud, and security (see the discussion in the preceding sections). A score card may be kept as to how many points were out of line compared to the total number tested. Perhaps the most important point to check however is if management and users were directly involved in the preinstallation effort, for such involvement goes a long way toward assuring success.

Generally speaking, it appears that auditors have paid too little attention to preinstallation activities. (This point was one of the conclusions in the recent SAC study mentioned previously.) If more organizations stressed this one last check before making a commitment, a great amount of trouble could be avoided. Evidently, not every organization can have all the necessary ingredients—competent people, internal discipline, systems for which there are no alternative processing methods, and money—to make the EDP effort a success. With the proper independent view provided by an early audit, many organizations might be able to realize this before it is too late.

To do a reasonable job in this regard, an auditor will have to keep up to date on what's happening in the computer field and also within the organization. This means continued study, not only in the form of reading and meetings but also through attending more formalized educational programs. For example, for anybody who wants to learn about the data base concept, there are one-hour lectures on that topic, full-week courses dealing with it in depth, and numerous books discussing it. Somewhere among all these offerings an auditor should be able to acquire the knowledge he needs in order to make a wise decision about a data base proposal.

If the auditor is called in during the preinstallation phase, he should take care not to delay any major decisions. Each major step requires a more costly commitment than the last one.

Thus if there is any chance that the auditor will recommend abandoning the venture or making major changes, such a decision should be communicated to management before proceeding to the next major area. Several specific questions the auditor should ask at this stage are:

- Did anyone, either internal or external, exert an unusual amount of pressure to cause action in a particular direction? Also, did anyone hold back relevant information that should have been volunteered?
- Was there a reasonable amount of management and user involvement? This should be ascertained by comparing what people actually did to what they were supposed to do according to the original plan.
- Did top managers delegate items to subordinates that they should not have delegated?
- Were source materials used properly to arrive at the conclusions?
- Is there adequate communication among users, management, analysts, and auditors? As the SAC report pointed out, management often thought that auditor involvement was at the 55 percent level whereas auditors in the same firms perceived their involvement to be at the 5 percent level. My conclusion is that management probably had been misinformed about the role the auditors played.
- Is the organization's value system appropriate? Is there an incentive to do an excellent job? Or is the value system set up to encourage people to be overcautious and conservative?

The point that brings up the issue here is a recent article telling that a data processing manager contracted to buy a used computer directly from a computer manufacturer for $650,000 when a comparable computer was available from another user for only $150,000. The manager used the excuse that top management had already approved a purchase at the higher amount, and now there was no need to make any waves by making any changes in the purchasing arrangement.

Here is a prime example of a person who did not have his employer's interest in mind, and he couldn't see any direct value to himself by creating a better deal for the firm. It is situations like this that should prompt one to make sure that management decisions are made by dedicated and responsible managers. If there is any question about the results one is getting, then it is time to get an auditor's independent opinion.

3

System Development

A data processing system may be viewed as involving two major activities. The first, which represents an occasional effort, is the design and installation of a system. The second is the day-to-day operation of a system once it is installed. From the standpoint of data processing personnel, there are different groups of people who work in each of those two areas. Users and auditors, however, should be involved with both areas.

The design of a business system includes the following steps:

1. Problem definition.
2. Analysis of the present manual or computerized system.
3. Planning of the procedures that will be used to process the data in the new system.
4. Report, file, and forms design.

The raw data for a business information system are generated from two sources: actual transactions and business plans. These raw data are processed to produce various reports that presumably help people perform their jobs. More specifically, the day-to-day operation of a system includes the following steps, each of which must be properly controlled so as to conform to the standards adopted by management.

1. Generation of the source data once a transaction has taken place or a plan has been formulated. The preparation of source data is usually a manual process; there are few instances where source data are automatically developed without human aid. Utility companies have experimented both with sending meter readings from customer sites over a telephone line back to the utility company and with picking up readings electronically by means of trucks equipped with sensors. But the basic method is still to have a person walk through the customer area and pick up the data manually on source documents. This segment of a system is usually the most expensive part of its operation, and it can also represent the source of most of the problems. In the typical EDP operation, the importance of source data generation is unfortunately often ignored because it takes place outside the walls of the computer center.

2. Moving the source data from where they are generated to the computer so that they can be processed. This may be handled either by company employees or, where appropriate, by contracted services such as the U.S. Postal System. If the data are directly generated in computer-readable form or converted to computer-readable form before reaching the computer center, they may be sent either over wires (installed by the organization itself or obtained from a telephone company) or physically in a form such as magnetic tape.

3. Converting the data to a form the computer can handle (unless they were generated in computer-readable form). While the latter style is growing in popularity, the former is still by far the more common. The most popular processes are keypunching of cards and key-stroking of magnetic tapes.

4. Checking all prior steps for errors, correcting the errors that are found, and reentering the corrections into the system. (A good portion of this book will concentrate on this area of control.)

5. Processing the data in the computer center. This involves such steps as sorting the data into various sequences, merging the data with other data, performing various calculations, up-

dating files, and preparing various reports to specification.
6. Distributing reports to the various users. This is usually accomplished by a physical distribution process.
7. Retaining and storing all data required for later use.

This chapter is concerned with the steps that must be followed in order to design a system that will result in those actions. While we will be concerned mostly with design at a higher level, we will occasionally get involved with some of the details of those steps.

GOALS OF SYSTEM DEVELOPMENT

Stated in the most general way, the goal of system development is to produce accurate systems that can perform in a timely fashion at a reasonable cost. As nice and reasonable as that statement sounds, general statements usually are not of much help in directing people in what they should do. Thus it would be desirable to establish more specific goals. The following guidelines should be useful in defining such specific goals, regardless of what kind of organization, functional area, or application is involved.

1. All systems should be designed expressly to serve people and to be operated by people. No situation should be allowed to occur where the desired system and the needs of people have to be altered to fit the idiosyncrasies of a computer or the whims of computer specialists, as was done in the following three cases:

> A customer of a bank sent in one check to cover the payments on both his mortgage and a personal loan. The bank sent the check back, asking for two separate checks. The customer did comply with that request, but as a consequence suffered a late-payment fee on the personal loan. (The bank provided only five days grace on personal loans but 15 days on mortgages.)
>
> In an effort to have up-to-date inventory information, a bookstore installed a computerized inventory control system. The system proved to be so much trouble to operate that sales

personnel in the store hated to see a customer come in; they knew that a sales transaction would create so much paperwork. The owners soon threw the computer out and just walked among the shelves when they wanted information as to what they had on hand.

A major credit card company enclosed a note with the following statement with all customer bills in mid-spring one year: "Vacation time is approaching, and many of you valued customers will be away for extended periods of time. Please arrange now to pay your credit card bill while you are away, since there is no way for our computer to handle your account in any other than the normal way for any length of time."

2. Each proposed system should have a predefined level of acceptability with respect to both accuracy and timeliness. For example, an inventory control system may be deemed acceptable if it leads to shipment of 90 percent of all customer orders within three days of receipt. Or an accounts receivable system could have as a goal a certain level of account turnover or an acceptable distribution of "slowness" in paying when the accounts are aged. Such acceptability goals must be realistic, however; you shouldn't expect—and probably can't afford—perfection. For example, you probably wouldn't want a zero rate of bad debts in a department store (however "perfect" that may sound at first), because that suggests you're turning away too many sales that would prove to be profitable.

3. All internal systems should have a return on investment of at least 15 percent. In calculating the return, if a benefit is truly intangible and can't be measured (such as improved morale), then no value should be attached to it. While it is recognized that some features will have a value that can't be measured, any benefit that comes from them will merely be used to offset certain costs—for example, system bugs or higher-than-expected inflation—that couldn't be or weren't considered at design time.

4. Systems involving external users (such as accounts-payable checks, the paying part of a payroll system, and regulatory requirements) can't be evaluated on a return-on-investment basis. The reason is that they are not operated for

internal information purposes, and thus the value they contribute can't be measured. Those systems are to have as a goal their development and operation at a minimum cost compatible with reasonable business practices. To some extent, a return-on-investment concept may be applied even here: the benefits of any changes to such systems have to stand up to the investment needed to get those benefits. Consider anything already spent on a system as irretrievable; the major money consideration is what will happen from now on.

5. Every system should reasonably safeguard not only organization assets but also the information developed within the system. This becomes the mandate for reasonable controls to be put into all systems. Make it known that the system will be audited to ensure that effective controls are indeed installed.

6. Give a low priority to any system that doesn't promise increased sales or reduced expenses, unless it is required by government or contract.

Specific goals along these lines might be developed by systems people or by users, but at some time should be confirmed by management and subsequently communicated to everyone.

Next, specific goals for each application must be developed. Here one must be careful not to state procedures instead of goals. For example, it is a *procedure* to key-verify the conversion of all source data; the goal is to end up with accurate source data. Stating goals in the proper, nonprocedural manner goes a long way toward ensuring that many alternative ways of doing the job will be considered.

The goal of a payroll system is to promptly reimburse employees for work performed, not to issue them paychecks every week. Note that the first version of the objective is more likely to bring about an innovative system such as that where payments are directly deposited into employee bank accounts.

The goals of a specific application ordinarily will be a compromise between those of users and management. While users may be inclined to spend more in order to achieve optimum results, management in the end has to pay the bill; therefore, it is essential that an agreement is reached on application-specific goals during this early phase.

DOCUMENTATION

Documentation is somewhat like the weather—everybody talks about it, but few seem to do anything about it. There are many articles and speeches that berate systems analysts for the quality and quantity (or lack) of their documentation. I will not add to that list here but instead offer some sound reasons for providing documentation and give some examples of documentation that should do the job well.

In its simplest version, documentation is a complete, hopefully legible, up-to-date record of everything that happened to put you where you are now. It is a good idea to develop some documentation standards and stay with them. The first standard simply is that there must be complete documentation. The second standard, or set of standards, relates to content and format. The reason for the latter is to enable people to find certain items quickly. For instance, knowing that a certain item of information is always in the same relative place on any form will cut down drastically on the time spent searching for it.

Documentation should begin by showing why a new system or a system change was considered. This should not require much space. Next, there must be an analysis of the present system. The present system might be shown in great detail, or it could be summarized in a brief report. The brief report style may be appropriate if there was never much doubt about going ahead with a new system *and* if it is clear that the new system will be designed essentially from scratch, without copying much of the existing system.

An important aspect of documentation is that it should help in establishing accountability. It would certainly be desirable to identify an analyst or user who is responsible for repeatedly designing systems that produce only a fraction of their "guaranteed" benefits. To do so, you must have kept records of what the new system was supposed to accomplish and how. Of course, any auditor reviewing the history of the system in order to establish such accountability must be able to tell what was and what wasn't within the control of the analyst.

SYSTEM DEVELOPMENT 73

Most systems today could be designed and/or operated largely from outside the organization as well as from inside. Documentation should support why the choice was made as it was. In those cases where company policy dictates the in-house solution, one sentence in the file will cover that point.

As an aside, it would be well to periodically report to management what such policies may be costing them. For example, some companies have a policy that payroll must be prepared internally. There is enough evidence now that service bureaus can do it with adequate control and possibly at a lower cost.

Much documentation will be prepared to explain to future analysts why certain things were done as they were. In future reviews of the system, it is much easier to update the first study than to start over from scratch. This works just as well for those proposed systems or proposed changes that never materialized. Let me illustrate with an example.

I was once assigned the job of developing a system that would provide a mailing list of certain people. In an early stage of establishing the job specification, I suggested to my manager that a person's name might appear like this on an envelope:

DOE JOHN

The manager said that format was not acceptable, since he didn't want recipients instinctively to know that the document had come from something as impersonal as a computer. In addition, he didn't want an account number to be printed anywhere on the envelope.

It soon became obvious to me that for some jobs the name and address file would have to be in alphabetical order by name, whereas for other jobs it would need to be in other sequences. Sorting to alphabetical order by last name would be simple if the last name were first in the name field (DOE JOHN), but it would be much more difficult if the first name had to be first (JOHN DOE).

So I had to develop a way that would sort alphabetically by

name whenever I wanted but would also provide for printing the name in the prescribed way. I could think of the following ways:

1. Put the person's name in the computer record in two different formats. For example, a record would contain the fields JOHN DOE, DOE JOHN, street name, and so on. In this way, the name as it first appears could be used for printing purposes, whereas the form in the second field would be used for sorting purposes. Note that under this method it costs a great deal more to enter the person's name into the file since it has to be keypunched twice. Also, more file space is required because of the additional characters for the duplicate name form.

2. Assign a numerical code to every name so that when the data are in numerical order, they are also in alphabetical order by name. For example, give Bob Aaron code 00005, Pete Zinger, code 99805, and so forth. Note that this method must carefully design the numeric code so there will be enough room for new names to be added. The time and the extra space required for handling the numeric code are less in total than for handling the redundancy in the first alternative.

I made a brief analysis of the time and cost differences between the two methods, assuming a system life of five years. Based upon that analysis, which was placed on record as part of the permanent system documentation, I chose to adopt alternative 2. The point is that, without documentation, people reviewing the system some years later might spend considerable time trying to establish the merits of my numerical code relative to other possible solutions, including the alternative rejected by me.

Barriers to Preparing Documentation

Despite the advantages to be gained by preparing and using documentation, apparently it is an area that is quite deficient. In my experience, there are more negative comments about documentation or its lack than about any other aspect of computer use.

There are some interesting reasons for this. Quite often the schedule for implementation of a system is somewhat optimistic. Or it may be a matter of so many changes being introduced while the latter stages of analysis or programming are underway. Thus when the due date for installation is right around the corner, there is a natural tendency to drop anything that can be dropped out without any apparent effect on implementation—and documentation is probably the foremost candidate.

Another barrier is that few people like to document. It is not particularly creative—the exciting part of the job has already been completed. It even appears unproductive. Perhaps the analyst or programmer had sketchy notes on paper or in his or her head, but has just not yet committed them to paper in a more formal way that can be retained. In short, documentation may appear to be no more than a copying process.

In some cases, people have flatly refused to provide documentation because they didn't want to. Particularly in times of high demand for computer specialists and a somewhat low supply, analysts and programmers have been able to use that excuse and get away with it.

Documentation can be looked upon in the same way as an insurance policy. It costs money to provide and seems to be a needless expense when you don't need it. But when you need it, it can become invaluable.

Probably the best way to avoid or overcome problems with establishing documentation is to get top management involved. Clearly point out the value and cost of documentation and the risk to which the company is exposed if there is no documentation. Get top management involved in the decision as to the level of documentation that will be used. Make a clear statement as to what management expects, and then follow through to see that it happens. If users are to be given the final authority for developing a system, then put documentation under their responsibility, too. Just don't allow a system to be implemented until the documentation is satisfactory.

STANDARDS

The terms *goal* and *standard* can easily become confusing. Although they are often used interchangeably, the terms have quite different meanings. Goals refer to the ends and results you want to reach; standards refer to the methods you use to get there.

In order to reach the various goals established for the system development phase, it will be necessary to adopt and enforce some strict standards. Probably the most important of them is that the proper levels of management be involved in the major aspects of system development, just as they were in preinstallation activities. The main tasks here are (1) setting priorities as to the order in which applications are reviewed for initial development and/or change and (2) making sure that the system proposal is sound before proceeding with the subsequent steps that will put it into operation.

The first and foremost consideration in system development is problem definition. As suggested before, if you have properly taken care of this point, you are half way to solution. In defining a problem, it is necessary to make a careful distinction between the problem and the symptoms of the problem. Occasionally it may turn out that a person is the problem. If the problem is so identified and verified, then only management should make a determination as to how much it will allow the bending of a system in order to endure the person.

The following guidelines may be useful in setting standards for the system development phase:

1. The goals of each system should be compatible with the goals of the organization. It is necessary to identify those situations where the goals of the people within an application are at odds with the goals of the system or of the organization. For example, some employees appear to have as their main goal continued employment, despite their complete lack of concern for corporate profits. Management must decide if it will allow that disparity to continue.

2. All activities should be controlled through time and cost budgets and reporting methods. In addition to feedback

SYSTEM DEVELOPMENT 77

through quantitative methods certain qualitative information should be made available. For example, the nature of complaints received and the relative standing with the media often provide information regarding the effectiveness of systems.

3. In designing any system, a company should look at least three to five years into the future. Designing a system to handle the current situation or only the immediate future just isn't cost-effective; that type of system may well be obsolete before it is ever installed. In order to meet this design standard, some of management's long-term plans will have to be made available to the people who design the systems. I believe this can be done in a reasonable way without the need for management to give away crucial organization secrets. (An acceptable exception to this standard is a system change to handle an emergency situation.)

4. All people affected by a system should participate in the system design and review. (This would normally be restricted to the supervisor level or higher.) A sign-off procedure should be used to assure that everyone knows and understands what has happened and what is to happen. This procedure establishes individual responsibility. The sign-off is not meant to necessarily signify concurrence, but only an understanding of the item being signed for. The use of a sign-off does not preclude the presentation of a minority position so long as it is objective and constructive.

5. There must be *system changes* when there are changes in methods of operation. Any system design that achieves merely a straight conversion from one method to another should not be permitted. Simple conversion doesn't accomplish much; usually there are some old steps that should be dropped. As a rule, any operating savings that might be gained from straight conversion don't pay for the cost of the design effort.

6. In any system conversion, existing controls (as a minimum) must be taken to the new system, except in those cases where it is proved that an existing control is not going to be cost-effective. In many cases, it appears that people quit using their common sense when it comes to establishing controls. For example, in a manually operated accounts-payable

system, a standard control demands that a person independent from the one preparing the checks must visually review all the checks prior to mailing them to vendors. Yet there have been automated systems in which the checks were mechanically stuffed into envelopes and sealed as soon as they came out of the printer on the first day the job was run; this was done before there was enough experience with the system to prove that it could handle the job accurately.

7. For all new systems and their major segments, there should be brainstorming sessions whose purpose is to anticipate problems that are likely to occur. For example, it was recently reported that one state has a major problem in its driver's license systems. The application was computerized in 1968; at that time a person's name became the major criterion for establishing a numeric code for each driver. Apparently, this was done because the person in charge felt that the clerical people involved could not get the job done using some other set of data. Even using other distinguishing features, such as a person's birthdate, numerous duplicate codes exist. Certainly the likelihood of this happening could have been predicted in 1968; a quick look at a few telephone books would have been sufficient.

8. The computer should be used to initiate transactions wherever practical. For example, when an inventory balance reaches a predetermined point, the computer system should generate the action that will reorder more. A computer system can be just as effective and well-controlled as its manual predecessor.

To what extent this standard will be applied depends on management. The decision may be to use computer initiation as far as possible across the board, or to use a varying approach in the different applications. Some managements may choose to have very little initiation by the computer. As mentioned before, internal standards are an individual matter.

9. Careful consideration must be given to the issue of *overrides*. In computer operations, there are many places where interaction between machine and operator is either necessary or desirable. For example, the computer may stop and request

immediate input from the operator as to what alternative route to take in the program. Similarly, such situations as incorrect files mounted or out-of-balance conditions may call for manual override. Having determined what, if any, overrides are appropriate, the next step is to decide which people should be authorized to override.

In a classic example of computer override, airline reservations clerks kept taking more seat reservations on a flight even though the computer indicated the flight was sold out. The result was that over 300 people showed up for a flight whose plane would hold 100. The system was relatively new, and personnel hadn't yet learned to trust it. Since the ticket clerks weren't aware of current events that were prompting so many reservations, they chose to override instead.

10. Sound business practices should be followed at all times, including such practices as:
Job rotation.
Individual performance evaluation.
Proper training at all levels on a timely basis.
Separation of duties to ensure internal control and efficiency.
Mandatory vacations.

11. One person on the staff should be designated as being responsible for keeping up to date on applicable *regulatory requirements*. Issues such as equal employment opportunity and personal privacy are so critical today as to make this a necessity in most organizations.

12. For each major segment of a system there must be complete and accurate documentation before the system is allowed to go into operation. At the system development level, the standard documentation package should include:
The reasons for considering a review of the existing system.
Any unusual items that were found in the review or any items that are likely to have some future impact on the revised system.
A system flowchart, sufficiently detailed to cover all operating aspects.
The economic justification for the system.
Detailed specifications for all computer programs.

Specific provisions for controls and an audit trail.

13. Once all parties involved in the system design have indicated their acceptance of the system specifications, the specifications should be considered frozen. The reason to have such a standard is to prevent the common practice of making changes in the system all the way through installation. Furthermore, adopting this standard will cause people to do a more thorough job of design, since they know they can't keep coming back to make minor changes.

CONTROLS

Controls over the system development phase should be in force to make sure that system development activities proceed as they should and to see that each resulting system meets the various standards that have been established.

The first step to be controlled is *problem definition*. This must include a clear definition of the purpose of the system. For example, does an inventory system exist to control reordering, to cost out sales, to aid in preparing financial statements, or to control theft? Unless that question is properly answered, the organization will have difficulties determining what its inventory control system should be like—or if in fact one is needed.

One way to control problem definition is to be certain to interview the subordinates in affected areas. The people who must make the system work are often an untapped source of helpful ideas. Also, brainstorming sessions may provide effective control. One of the results of the problem definition phase should be a clear conclusion as to whether or not a computerized system is needed.

Once controls are in operation to make sure systems are designed only when they should be, then there must be a set of controls whose purpose is to make sure the required systems are designed properly.

Analysis of a present system can become a runaway process

SYSTEM DEVELOPMENT 81

if it isn't carefully controlled. There is a great chance that an analyst will try to study everything about a present system unless the goal and the scope of the analysis have been clearly established in advance. The applicable control, therefore, is a clear-cut statement (a "shopping list") of what is needed, along with a realistic timetable for the analysis.

In an overall sense, the soundest control is regular management review of what is happening. This means that the documentation of systems development activities has to be up to date. This documentation, which should be saved for an indefinite period of time, must be supplemented with progress reports showing how the time and money spent on the project compare with the original budgets.

Without such regular review, management will be unable to react or act as the situation calls for. During the system development phase, it may often be necessary to move people in or out of the project, to provide more money so as to stay on schedule, or to extend due dates. In more extreme cases, a quick management decision to abandon the entire project or to replace people may be essential.

A second level of control is going to be that which is exercised by users. At a minimum, users would require reasonably complete sketches of reports and source documents and firm ideas about data flow, controls, timing, and costs. This follows the idea in the previous section that ultimate responsibility for making a system work should lie with the user.

The Audit Trail

No discussion of auditing would be complete without introducing the topic of the audit trail. The term audit trail has unfortunately taken on the wrong meaning. It almost sounds as if special procedures have to be set up to satisfy the demands of auditors. This is generally not the case, since auditors aren't likely to require any procedures that management and owners wouldn't want as a part of normal operation.

That possible confusion has led some people to use the term *management trail*. But this may suggest that management is going to come along to check on something, which is not so likely to happen often either. Thus the term *transaction trail* may be more appropriate. It refers to the procedures that permit users to trace forward from source data to completed reports or to work backward from completed reports to source data. Clearly, these procedures receive much more attention from users in the day-to-day operation of the system than from either managers or auditors.

It is unconscionable to imagine that anyone would be happy with a system that could create a balance in a file or a number on a report without enabling users to see readily, without excessive manipulation, what specific transactions created that amount. In any event, one of the techniques used by auditors is to attempt to follow the transaction trail in order to see how to get from one point to another in the system.

Because of changes in computer technology and the desire to use different (and sometimes cheaper) methods to get jobs done, the transaction trail is quickly changing. For example, a manual system often provides for complete detail of an account balance for a period extending over several years; a computer system will probably have such detail only for the current period. Source data in a manual system are prepared manually; the computer itself may authorize transactions and document them by printing an appropriate list upon request. Despite the changes that are taking place in the transaction trail, it can't be allowed to disappear.

Backup

No matter how well a system has been designed so as to prevent the loss of information or equipment, things will go wrong and there will be a need to use backup features. Backup merely refers to the means of recovering from a loss; it is needed for data, equipment, programs, and procedures. (It is assumed that provision has been made for backup personnel, just as in the prior manual systems.)

Data backup. This is generally handled by copying files at scheduled times and then storing the duplicates at another site.

The off-site location may be another facility of the same organization, a vault in the firm's bank, or a site maintained by a firm that is in business to provide such a service. Quite often the last method uses space in a carefully guarded and controlled underground environment. Copying data in this manner and taking it to the storage site obviously has its cost. But most firms treat the cost of providing backup as an insurance premium—the cost is rather nominal compared to the cost of a disaster for which there has been no provision for prompt recovery. Source data and some reports need to be protected as well. This is typically done through the use of microfilm; it is accomplished less often by storing duplicate copies of the data in paper form.

Equipment backup. Some organizations are large enough to provide their own backup equipment. Many large firms have more than one computer. Typically, the computers are exact (or close) duplicates so that there is no problem running a program on either machine because of feature incompatibility. A company with a real-time system will often have duplicate facilities in order to avoid being down due to machine failure. This is common in the airline seat reservation business. In any situation, the backup may be provided by having a formal arrangement with another organization.

Program backup. Although programs should not get lost, apparently they occasionally do. The best control to recover from such an event is to have copies stored elsewhere. Not only should duplicates of programs be saved in a computer-readable form such as on tape or disc, it may also be good to save a printed copy of the program. If worse comes to worst, at least you could keypunch the instructions from the listing.

Procedure backup. Procedures will occasionally need to have a backup. Suppose, for example, you have some version of an on-line system or perhaps a real-time system that does not have duplicate equipment backup. When the equipment fails, you may want to have some sort of alternative system that can be used until the regular system is operational again. This situation hopefully won't have to last too long; using such a backup procedure soon becomes extremely awkward, especially if people can't get at the data in the files. Some companies take a calculated risk that this won't happen too often or for too long and temporarily close down the operations affected rather than provide for a backup procedure.

Tied directly to all the above points about backup is the situation created by a disaster such as a fire, flood, or similar occurrences that essentially destroy the primary method of operation, forcing the organization to go to a backup. What is needed here is a carefully detailed disaster recovery plan. In a classical example, a firm's only copy of its recovery plan burned up when its computer center caught fire. As might be imagined, the new system calls for several copies of the plan to be stored in different locations, a couple of them in the homes of key executives.

AUDITING SYSTEM DEVELOPMENT ACTIVITIES

Auditing of the system development phase should focus on two issues: (1) how well the development activities were carried out, and (2) how well the resulting system can be expected to work. A proper job done at this stage will go a long way toward ensuring that the next steps in the design effort will proceed well.

This particular audit must be completed promptly so that any necessary changes can be made quickly. In any event, it should be completed before the next step begins; otherwise, there will be efforts needlessly spent, or there may be a tendency to go ahead with a poor system merely to protect the money that has already been spent.

Accuracy

An audit of the accuracy aspect of system development is concerned with two things: (1) the accuracy with which the development study was completed, and (2) the projected accuracy of the system once it is operating.

With respect to the first task, the audit will be concerned with following up on all the activities to make sure that sound, representative data were used; that any assumptions made were reasonable and not farfetched; that cost and timing estimates were reasonable; and that no major, necessary tasks were overlooked. In this process, it is obviously necessary to double-check all quantitative data contained in the study.

Regarding the projected accuracy of a system's operation, we have all heard many horror stories about the problems involved in getting a system to perform the way it should. I will relate just one actual situation here. One major credit card company discovered that in a particular year it had paid airlines $15 million more for charged tickets than what it had charged its cardholders. The control that was missing was a comparison of the total bills being sent to customers with total purchases from vendors. Unfortunately for the company, this wasn't discovered until several years later. By then some of the cardholders couldn't be located, and others just ignored the bill because it was so after-the-fact. While it is difficult to imagine how a system could be designed that lacked such a basic control, this one obviously did. In the meantime, the company couldn't understand why it was operating at a loss.

Essentially we are concerned here that all valid transactions are handled completely. We want to make sure that invalid transactions don't enter the process and that no transactions get lost. Furthermore, we want all processing steps to proceed according to a good plan. We don't want good data to deteriorate through later errors, such as transcription. In addition, source data transactions must be processed against the proper master records. (Accounts-payable checks are to be sent to companies from which purchases were made, not to others whose names just happened to be in the file.)

To make system accuracy possible within reasonable limits, a lengthy list of controls has been developed. The names of some of the techniques are key-verification, record counts, batch totals, hash totals, and self-checking digits. They are described later in some detail.

At some point it is necessary for users, EDP specialists, and auditors to become familiar with the types and expected rates of errors. Appropriate controls that will help establish the desired level of accuracy must then be chosen for each error type. Care must be taken not only to use controls that will indeed be effective but also to weigh the cost of each control against its expected benefits. Furthermore, there must be some consideration of the ability of employees to bypass the use of controls as they were meant to function. For example, assume the computer has been programmed to stop when a specified error is detected; the value of that control is forgone if the computer operator can simply push the start button to resume processing.

The auditing technique that will be most effective here is to review the documentation, specifically, the system flowchart. Hopefully, the system flowchart will be detailed enough to provide answers to questions such as:

- Will the output of a system correspond precisely to the transactions that had been entered previously? That is, can we be sure no transactions were lost, gained, or processed twice?
- If some errors are detected at a particular control spot, where are they corrected and by whom? Also, are the corrections subject to the same editing process that caught the errors originally (or perhaps to an even stricter process)?
- If employee X should be absent due to illness or should leave the organization, what is there to assure that the replacement will be competent, trained, and motivated to properly take over the position?

It is "what if" questions like these that need to be adequately answered. Hopefully most of these have been considered at design time and have been reasonably provided for in the design.

Unfortunately, an auditor cannot always rely on the study of system flowcharts, since they may be sketchy or nonexistent, so there must be another approach to review the provisions for

SYSTEM DEVELOPMENT 87

accuracy. One alternative source which should provide some answers is the manpower estimates. These estimates should include some documentation indicating how many people operate the basic system; how many (or who) will be involved with controls; and who will be concerned with corrections. From this documentation, it should soon become obvious if the latter two aspects—controls and error correction—have received sufficient attention to ensure system accuracy.

Efficiency

Most of the problems involving efficiency will probably fall in the area of overly optimistic forecasts of what the proposed system will achieve. This often occurs as a result of overenthusiasm or because of an assumption that the boss wanted to hear something "good" as opposed to the truth, which tends to be less spectacular.

The auditor will not only have to be intimately familiar with all the EDP equipment, but also have relevant knowledge of each application and the kinds of people who will be operating it. The backgrounds of those making the proposal will be important, too. Some people will have to be double-checked carefully; in the case of others, their word can be readily accepted.

Fraud

It is unlikely that a fraudulent system was ever set up with fraud in mind at the time of design. It is my suspicion that fraud is always an afterthought once the system is underway. In fact, of all the frauds brought to light, few were caused by the systems analyst; most were perpetrated by the user. (This point may be considered a counterargument to my earlier point about having the user be responsible for the system.)

In light of this, the major task is to make sure the operation of the system will not later deteriorate to the point where fraud can be committed. Many of the features that control accuracy also act to control fraud, since acts of fraud tend to throw relationships out of balance or create situations that are hard to justify. When such a situation is found, the auditor should pursue the matter far enough to conclude that it is either fraud or an unusual result which can reasonably be explained.

Security

Many security problems can be traced directly to the system development phase. Quite often the needed steps are omitted here either as a result of a simple oversight or because analysts recognized that to include them would have an undesirable impact on cost estimates. The idea is that even if the deficiency is later discovered, it can always be corrected at that time. But we know that it is so much easier to go on to new things later, and we typically never get around to cleaning up problems left over from before. Furthermore, by the time the deficiency is discovered, disaster may have occurred.

In determining what security measures have been provided, system flowcharts may at times be useful. For example, some of the processes involving data backup may be shown on a system flowchart. Most security controls, however, are not the kind of thing that would ever be shown on a system flowchart. Many security features are part of the internal workings of a program or are related to the operation of the computer (for example, the manner in which switches are set). Both aspects are somewhat more detailed than the design of a system at the flowchart level.

Looking at this problem another way, there are application controls and general controls. Application controls are specific steps designed for a particular application, and in most cases are reflected in the system flowchart. For example, one may key-verify the conversion of payroll source data but use the batch-total method to verify the conversion of inventory data; either method will be listed on the system flowchart.

By contrast, general controls apply across all applications. For example, a lock on the computer center door is a general control, as is the installation of smoke/fire detectors, but neither would appear on any flowchart. Since most security

SYSTEM DEVELOPMENT 89

controls are general rather than application-oriented, an auditor must look beyond the system flowchart level. Careful review of the documentation and interviews with all the people involved, useful as they may be, do not always produce convincing evidence that all aspects of the security system will really work in an emergency. The only true test is to simulate a situation to see for yourself. Thus the auditor might walk in unannounced with statements such as these:

The master payroll file can't be located. What is done to obtain the backup copy in a prompt fashion?

The computer has just gone down during the payroll run. Find out from the company across town if you can drop in on them within a few hours to complete your payroll on their machine. (Don't just talk about this. Go there and try to do it; you'll soon find out how good the backup arrangement with them is.)

The disc file containing programs has just been wiped out. How do we get a duplicate?

A fire has just started in the CPU and is spreading quickly. Who does what? (If there isn't some evidence of organization, you know that the disaster plan may not have been set up well, and the personnel may not have been well trained.)

Tests such as these should not take much time and would hardly create great costs. Top management should certainly endorse the idea, for the knowledge gained about all the reactions (good or bad) should be invaluable.

Effectiveness

System analysis and design call for a number of fairly clear and distinct steps to be performed. Because these steps are quite predictable, they can in principle be scheduled, if not in terms of the exact time needed for each step, then at least in terms of their sequence.

Since the purpose of a system is to provide information, the first step is to identify the people, or perhaps the job positions, in need of information. Next to be determined is precisely what information they need to perform their work effectively; that is, report content and format must be defined and fixed. When we know what results people need, then we can determine what raw data are needed. After this we develop the processes that take the raw input data and convert them to the required results as defined earlier. Finally, having formed a firm idea of how quickly results are needed, we can determine what kinds of processes must be used to satisfy timing requirements.

Since so much depends on how the system is designed, this phase must be particularly well controlled. The technique needed here is to review each step and get it approved by users before proceeding to the next. No matter how well an analyst likes an idea, it just won't work when installed unless users have been turned on to it.

A key point to consider at design time is whether a system appears to be properly integrated with the others to which it relates. No system exists without some direct impact upon another system, and if there is poor or no integration, then either excessive cost will be required to relate them or the value of the relationship may be forgone.

Consider the following situation, which occurred at a major bank. In 1958 the bank computerized its checking accounts. Customer account numbers were designated to be eight numeric characters. Once the checking accounts were operating smoothly, savings accounts were computerized. This time, customer identification codes used the account holder's Social Security number—a nine-digit code. Several years later the bank decided to automate all its mortgages and other long-term loans. Because of the wish to break down all loan accounts in many different ways, the decision was made to use a 14-digit account number.

The result: three systems working independently of one another, each of them using its own account-numbering method, and each with its own set of files.

Then the inevitable happens. Management states that it wants to start getting information about how much business it does with any specified customer. There is no automated way to get that information because there is no common thread among the three files.

The following situation, described to me by a bank auditor, is another example of poor integration. The bank where he worked would not bounce a reasonable-size check of one of its good-standing customers if that customer also had a savings account at the bank. Each morning an officer at the bank would get a pile of checks about to be bounced, and he would match them one at a time to a list of savings accounts. A "bad" check for a savings customer would be honored; those checks for whom no manual match could be made would be returned NSF ("non-sufficient funds").

There seems to be a trend in banks to redesign to the extent necessary to interrelate such central activities. While there may have been a justification for designing independently a number of years ago, there probably isn't now. Thus we can all learn a lesson from the above about the need for integration.

The need to ensure proper integration is another reason for auditors to be called in at design time.

INVOLVEMENT OF MANAGEMENT, USERS, AND AUDITORS

It appears that many automated systems have been designed almost solely by computer specialists. Perhaps there would be nothing wrong with that approach if a good job were being done of it. In many cases, though, the results have been detrimental to the total organization. The most common complaint is that users get much information they don't need but at the same time fail to get other information they could use to great advantage.

Generally speaking, computer specialists are not expert enough in all the functional areas of an organization to design systems for them without extensive assistance from users, management, and auditors. In particular, problem definition and the establishment of information requirements, both of which are crucial parts of the system design, cannot be left to computer specialists.

Users probably must accept some blame here, too. Some have been heard to say, "Give me what you think I need." Nor is management free of blame. Too often management backs off after having done no more than approve the spending of certain sums of money. A likely reason is that management deems computers and those who work with them too technical to be managed like any other functional area. But this deficiency can be overcome by spending a minimum amount of time in a computer concepts course. I have seen hundreds of managers and executives ready to accept the normal responsibility of managing computer specialists after 15 to 20 hours of concentrated instruction.

Historically, auditors have been somewhat reluctant to get involved at the design stage. The major reason given is that the auditor would lose the needed independence if he were later to audit a system in which he had played a role in designing. I have several comments on that point.

First, it might be better to have lost a little independence than to end up with some of the freakish, uncontrolled systems that we have all seen. It is unlikely that many of those systems would have gotten off the drawing board if an auditor had seen them earlier. Second, an auditor could be involved in system design up to a point, such as being concerned with setting standards and giving a general concept about the controls needed. There is no need to get involved with detail design. Third, an auditor could stay with the design all the way, and a different auditor could perform the later audit. The auditor involved in design work could either be a hired auditor or a person who had auditor savvy.

Certain recent developments should dispel most of the reluctance to get involved in system design. Both the AICPA (representing external auditors) and the IIA (representing internal auditors) have adopted certain guidelines that spell out how the involvement can take place. Furthermore, CPA firms have their own MAS (Management Advisory Services) divisions; their major function is to help clients design business systems.

Apparently, some auditors hide behind the "independence" argument in order to cover up for their lack of adequate knowledge about computers. Hopefully such auditors can be identified and given the proper training. This naturally assumes that they have the interest and the aptitude to learn.

An internal auditor may not have been involved in the design of a system simply because he didn't know about the effort or wasn't invited to participate. If this is the case, there appears to be a personnel problem.

We could go on handing out blame for noninvolvement, but it is more productive to treat the topic in a positive manner. I think the solution is rather simple: it is a matter of education. Clearly show all parties—management, users, and auditors—why their participation is needed, and carefully point out the consequences of noninvolvement. It seems to be a fact of life, for instance, that if users aren't sufficiently involved, they tend to design and operate their own system. Then both systems operate independently at the same time, causing excessive costs and creating other obvious problems.

A question that must be addressed in the involvement matter is who is ultimately responsible for the system. I think the answer to this question is, without any qualifications, the user. It certainly isn't the EDP department, which, unlike the user, actually spends only a fraction of its time on any one application. Many organizations have a hard time accepting this fact and an even harder time adapting to it. In many cases, users would have to upgrade their technical and managerial competence considerably in order to live up to that responsibility.

4

Computer Program Development

A computer program is a set of instructions that tells the computer what to do. It serves the same purpose as the written or verbal instructions to a person who has to handle the human parts of a system. A major difference is that the computer does what you tell it, within its capability, whereas a person willfully may or may not follow instructions or may interpret instructions incorrectly.

Once a system has been designed and exists at the system flowchart level, a program has to be written (or otherwise obtained) to provide for each computer run on the system flowchart. Figure 7 shows a system flowchart that requires five computer programs. Number two, called a file update, is probably the most difficult of the five. Number one, the sort, is a general program to which specific parameters are fed for each sort.

Developing workable programs involves several major steps: preparation of a program flowchart; translating the steps on the program flowchart into detailed instructions written in a user-oriented language such as COBOL or FORTRAN; converting the programmer's language to machine language; and testing and debugging the program to make it usable.

Figure 7. A sample systems flowchart (partial).

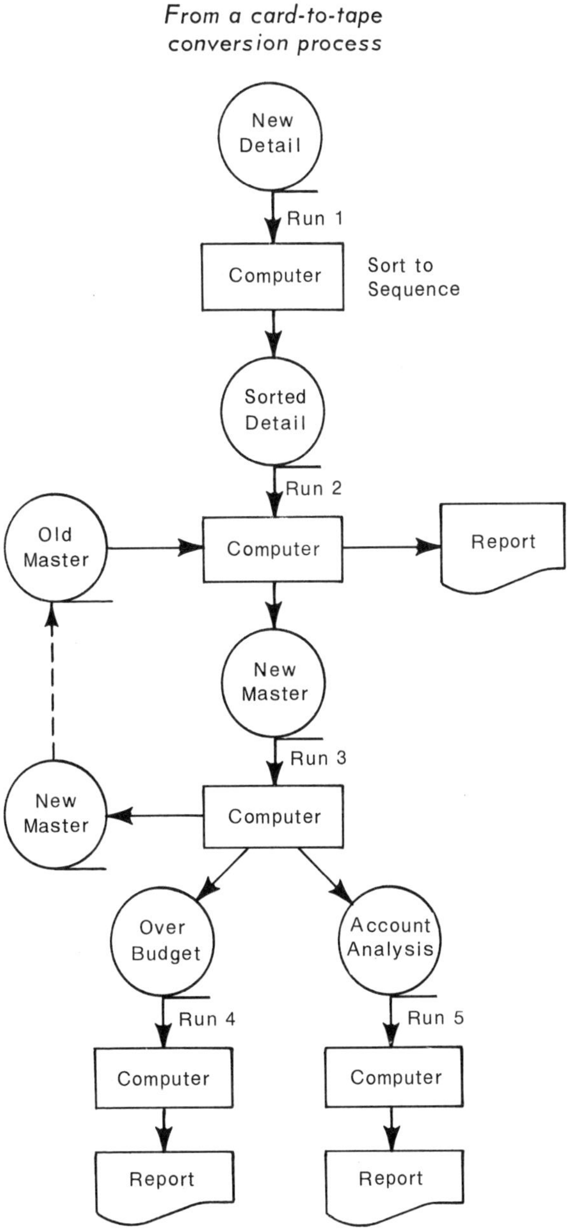

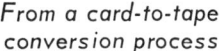

GOALS

The goals of computer program development may be viewed as threefold:

1. To correctly manipulate input data to produce output as prescribed by various parts of system development.
2. To include steps that will either prevent, catch, or flag obvious errors that might have occurred in any part of the system, including manual operations.
3. To keep each program flexible enough so that minor changes can be made without a major rewrite of the program.

While these goals may seem simple enough to describe, the brief history of computer use has shown that they are not that simple to reach. For one thing, qualified programmers are not plentiful. A particular mental capacity is needed to be a programmer; the percentage of people with the appropriate mental makeup might range around 1 to 2 percent. And considering that many of those who are mentally qualified do not want to become programmers, it is easy to see that the field is quite constricted.

Another problem in reaching these programming goals is that many users find it difficult to communicate to programmers what they want and how they want it done. Related to this problem is the fact that users, no matter how experienced in dealing with a present system, are rarely able to think of all the necessary items that have to be made known to systems analysts and programmers.

Users who do have the ability to describe their work to programmers in reasonable detail and clarity may not want to do so for several reasons. First, they may fear the loss of their jobs if the work should become computerized. Second, describing what they do, in the detail necessary, may indicate that their functions aren't very important. Finally, some people are just too stubborn to provide the needed help.

Some program changes that are clearly called for may not be

provided because too much effort, cost, and system disruption would be involved.

STANDARDS

Although some phases of programming are commonly believed to be highly creative and, by implication, rather unpredictable, many standards can be developed that will direct programmer efforts so as to serve the organization effectively. An obvious standard for all programs is that each one should do what it is supposed to do. This includes making sure the results are in the proper format and detail requested by the intended recipient. If system development was a bit shaky on this point, here is the last good place to set it right.

Program Flowcharts

Since programming generally starts (or should start) with a program flowchart, that is the logical starting point for some standards. In fact, requiring a program flowchart may itself be considered a standard. There should be some prescribed methods of preparing a program flowchart, such as starting at the upper left corner of a sheet and generally working to the right and down.

It is a good idea to use common symbols within an organization, preferably those adopted by the American National Standards Institute (ANSI) in 1966. (These standards have been used in all the flowcharts in this book.) In previous years, computer and forms vendors freely gave out plastic templates of flowcharting symbols. There was little uniformity among those symbols (for example, one might use a circle as a sort symbol, another, two triangles abutted to each other), but many of them are still in use. Such lack of standards means that it will take more time to figure out what a flowchart means, despite the fact that a descriptive term may appear in or next to the symbol.

Editing Programs

Quite often the first time source data are processed by the computer is in an editing run. This particular type of program tests the data to see if each item or the total aggregate meets certain criteria. (See the section on controls later in this chapter for a more detailed discussion.) Some of the hundreds of possible points tested by such programs are:

Is each data field complete?
Are there any alphabetic characters in fields that should contain only numeric characters? Are all amounts reasonable in size?

An edit program can go a long way toward catching errors that would cause a lot of distress if they got past this point. Applicable standards are:

The edit program should indicate error conditions clearly by using words and terms instead of codes that have to be looked up, learned, or memorized. It is important that such errors be caught soon.
The system itself should allow for the steps (most likely manual) that would correct the errors and provide for the corrections to be reentered.
Resubmissions should be subjected to the same (or possibly a stricter) editing process as the original source data.

Programming Languages

Another important programming standard is the selection of the particular language to be used. Some computer centers carefully match the language to the nature of the problem. This makes for the most effective way of preparing the program and may also maximize computer running efficiency; however, it generally requires that programmers know how to use several different languages.
Other computer centers stick with just one language. This

approach may require much ingenuity in accomplishing some functions, in addition to having an adverse effect on machine running time. On the other hand, programmers don't have to learn so much and aren't bothered with having to forget about one language when attempting to use another.

Perhaps a more important programming standard concerns the nature of a language itself. Is the language designed to standards adopted by a reasonable number of computer manufacturers? If the answer is yes, then the programs you have written can be run on another computer with minimum rewriting. If not, then perhaps a program has to be completely rewritten when a different computer is used, which is certain to happen at some future time.

PROGRAM WRITING

While at times it may seem that most of the activity in developing a system is the writing of the programs, actually this phase probably represents only 10 to 20 percent of the total time. (In fact, if my earlier suggestion to spend considerably more time on system development is followed, then the percentage devoted to programming will be even less.) What seems to throw programming time out of proportion is the time needed to debug programs; this activity could take more time than that required for the original writing. Many of the problems related to debugging reflect programmer competence. (Actually, it may be difficult to clearly determine where writing leaves off and debugging begins, since a program is rarely ever complete when it is first tested—as soon as errors of commission are detected, it is usually noted there have been errors of omission.)

Some Pitfalls

It is essential that the computer be used to do the work that is appropriate for it. Unfortunately, programs are not always designed that way. There is no excuse for practices such as the following:

- Printing a report that shows an actual amount and a budget amount and then expecting the reader to make the calculation which would produce a variation.
- Printing a variation only in dollars when providing a percentage difference as well would be more helpful.
- Showing individual values as a percentage of the total but then not having the percentages adding to 100 just because the programmer didn't take the same level of care in writing the program that a person would be likely to take in making the calculations manually.
- Printing a report from which users have to take adding machine tapes to get needed totals.
- Printing data on a report in a vertical fashion when users need those data in horizontal form.

Programs should be written so that they not only provide reasonable answers but run in a time frame that is appropriate. For example, on a bill to a customer, you don't want the minimum payment to be an amount greater than the total amount due. Nor do you want a customer bill to show a due date that is earlier than the day the customer gets the bill.

Who Should Do It?

There is no reason to assume that all programming has to be done in-house by employees. An alternative is to buy a package of programs for an application already written by someone else. Packages applicable to all major business functions are available from most computer manufacturers and from dozens of software houses. The use of a package is more common in smaller organizations, where computer power is required but the user wants to avoid the need to hire and retain computer specialists.

Of course, there are some pitfalls in this method, the major one being that the package may be somewhat general and not tailored to all your needs. Here is where a careful cost-benefit study should be made. Perhaps you can afford to give up some features if you can get by with a much lower cost. After all, users can't expect to get everything they want; at some point the law of diminishing returns will apply.*

Another interesting approach that should be considered is to farm out some of the work. Generally, the most undesirable part of programming is the coding of the instructions. If a software vendor has a roster of people who are satisfied (at least temporarily) to work as pure coders, consider taking advantage of it. The user would design the system in the usual manner, making sure to include reasonable controls. Then the user would clearly establish the specifications to be used by the vendor in writing the detailed instructions, and later determine that those specifications had been followed.

If for any reason the organization has a policy against farming this kind of work out, now is a good time to reexamine the validity of that policy.

PROGRAM TESTING AND DEBUGGING

Types of Errors

Writing a program of any significance (and that suggests a certain length) involves so much detail and so many possible directions to go that it is almost impossible to avoid errors. These errors may be of the commission type or the omission type, although the latter is more likely to occur. The four most typical causes of program errors are:

1. *Errors at system development time.* For example, if employees' travel-expense reimbursements are to be made on the weekly paycheck, income tax will be withheld on the expense reimbursement portion unless it has been made clear during the development phase that the amount is to be treated as an "other" item and not as taxable income.

2. *Errors in logic while preparing the program flowchart.* The logic needed in a program for inventory replenishment, for

---

* Interesting evaluations of program packages can be found in "User Ratings of Software Packages," *Datamation,* each December issue.

example, could get quite complex. As a result, too much or too little inventory could easily be ordered. This particular type of error is likely to be the most difficult to find and correct since it is hard to get another person to help debug logic. Two people will take such different approaches to a problem that it becomes difficult for the nonwriter to relate to what the writer has done.

3. *Selection of an incorrect instruction code.* For instance, the use of the word PRINT in an instruction instead of WRITE could cause all kinds of interesting results, the most predictable being an ERROR message. Fortunately, the computer can detect and report many errors in this category.

4. *Errors in entering the program into the computer.* Programs are generally entered in one of three ways: (1) punching of IBM cards, (2) key-stroking instructions to magnetic tape or disc, or (3) keying directly from a typewriter into the computer. In each case, somebody must read the instructions from a sheet of paper and enter them on a keyboard. Quite often this is done by a person other than the programmer; in any event, keying errors can easily occur.

The purpose of debugging is to locate and correct these errors. If an error appears to be of type one or two, particular care should be taken to find the exact cause. You may think you have it corrected only to find that it is still causing trouble somewhere else.

Test Methods

At some point the program will at least run through the computer—it will be acceptable in a "clerical" or "mechanical" (electronic) sense, if not in a logical or processing (job output) sense. The next step is to test it with some data, first with some routine, perhaps hypothetical transactions, and then perhaps with live data from a recent period. This phase is likely to uncover errors involving all four types described above, so more searching and corrections are ordinarily needed.

These initial program tests are performed by the programmer himself. Once the programmer says that a program is ready to go, additional tests should be performed by someone else, preferably an EDP auditor. It is essential that such testing be done before the program becomes operational, since by that time it will be more difficult to make corrections in it.

One test method the auditor might apply would be to actually audit the program step by step to see what it does. To do so, the auditor would presumably work with the program specifications, the program flowchart, and perhaps a list of the coded instructions.

This method, though at one time considered to have excellent potential, is rarely used in actual practice. One difficulty in using it is that many auditors lack either the ability or the interest to conduct such an intensive program analysis. Even if an auditor were inclined to try, it can become quite difficult to try to follow another person's logic—there are as many ways to solve a problem as there are people. Also, there is the problem of making sure that the version of the program being reviewed is the one that is actually used. Finally, alternative methods may do just as good a job at considerably less expense.

The best alternative method is the use of test data made up by the auditor. These data are often referred to as a test deck, for the simple reason that not many years ago, such data would have been represented by a deck of punched cards (in some cases, they still are).

A key to the use of test data is to include not only all valid types of data but also some invalid types. You want to know what the computer will do with bad data as well as good data. Also, you must be careful that there is a proper amount of data. For example, if a program is supposed to check if there are too many transactions of a certain type, then put in whatever constitutes "too many" such transactions to see what the results are.

Of course, the ultimate test is whether the program will work with live data. (If a system is completely new, there may not yet be any live data.) When testing a program with live data, make sure you're using *true source data* rather than data in which all source errors have been corrected.

There are two major problems with using live data for a program test. One, such data may not contain everything you want to check for. Two, it can become quite costly to conduct a valid check because such a great volume of data may be required.

If the test deck method is used, the kinds of items you might want to place in your test data are:

1. Unusual amounts, both small and large, negative and positive.
2. Duplicate transactions when there is supposed to be only a single transaction for any account.
3. Transactions out of sequence.
4. Incomplete records, with either characters missing in fields or some complete fields missing.
5. Data that require certain logical relationships, including cross-footing.

The use of test data has some drawbacks. First, it takes time to prepare the data. Second, effective test data can't be prepared without knowledge of the program specifications. Third, the method requires a certain amount of computer time, probably at a time when available computer hours are in short supply.

Another simple test of a program is a review of real-life results. If some responsible person would just fan through printed reports, a lot of erroneous data would never get out the door. For example, this technique would have saved an amusement company a lot of trouble: their computer prepared 600 identical bingo cards.

DOCUMENTATION

I have already commented on people's lack of desire to document their work. It should be clear that program documentation doesn't exist only to show, after the fact, how a program was written. It may also be essential to the writing of a program in the first place.

Ideally, the documentation of system development should indicate clearly what each program in a system is supposed to do. If such detailed documentation has in fact been provided, it would be well to include a copy of it in the program files. If not, then something of that type must be prepared now and made available to the programming staff. The reason is very simple: a good program cannot be written unless there is a clear indication of its objectives.

Besides this list of objectives there should be a clear indication of what the available input is and what the output should look like. Also, the sources of input and the desired distribution of output should be documented at this stage, since it would be helpful if the computer programs contained this information.

The bulk of the documentation for the program development phase should clearly show how each program was prepared. The minimum documents are a program flowchart and a list of each program in its coded form. Notes and comments on tough spots or why something was handled in a certain way are also useful. When such notes and comments are used, it is desirable to do it in such a way that they can easily be carried over to revised versions of the documentation. Generally, the best method is to embed them in the program itself rather than list them separately. Such comments in programs are for the use of people only; the computer simply skips over them when executing the programs. They add clarity at practically no extra processing cost. Furthermore, program flowcharting provides for an "annotation" symbol to serve a similar purpose with regard to the logic. It should be an internal standard that both forms of documentation are used to an appropriate degree.

The programming documentation should also include specific instructions to the computer operator. This would include such things as where input is to come from; the particular files to mount (such as reels of tape or disc packs); the kind of paper to load into the printer; and the kinds of things that would cause the execution of the program to halt prematurely. An idea as to what the printed output should look like can also be useful. If the operator has a sample of the intended output at the beginning of the job, ineffective runs can be avoided. When the operator sees that something is wrong at the beginning of the job, the computer can be stopped and the problem corrected. And even if a job is run all the way through, a review before sending it can avoid the need for users to examine and reject obviously inadequate output.

The part of writing a program that can seemingly be avoided is the preparation of a program flowchart. Although most of my work is with college students, I suspect the same situation is true of programming practitioners. Most people want to go straight to the coding of instructions in a programming language and avoid the program flowchart.

Some current programming environments make it easy to get away with that. If a programmer is programming and testing in an on-line mode, he or she may be able to try various solutions without leaving much of a trail as to how many errors were made in how many tries. Thus programming management may not be fully aware of how much programmers are floundering about because they aren't using standard methods of program writing.

With computer hardware becoming somewhat cheaper and programmer costs rising, it may be becoming more practical to permit programmers to use the computer to debug programs, that is, to let the programmer make many tries at a program and to quickly make a few, perhaps hasty, changes on the basis of various error codes generated by the computer. But at some point this approach becomes too costly, and the programmer should go back to the drawing board and tackle the conceptual base of the program—and that means the program flowchart.

Some programmers have told me the only way they can do a complicated job is to code the instructions first and then prepare the flowchart. Of course I don't really believe that, nor do I approve of that sequence of steps to get a working program. At some point we must rely upon the programmer's supervisor to make sure that a proper and efficient job is being done.

CONTROLS

The application of controls in computer program development involves two wide areas: (1) controlling the program development process itself, and (2) the controls to be built into the computer programs. From the auditor's standpoint, it is necessary to determine what any control is supposed to achieve and if in fact it works as planned or if programmers or operators have figured out ways to bypass it.

Traditionally, programming was considered to be too specialized, creative, or even artistic to be controlled; however, that philosophy is gradually disappearing, and programming is beginning to be subjected to the same controls as other business functions.

With regard to the development process itself, a schedule is needed which shows what is to be completed at what time. Then it is up to the programmer's supervisor or project leader to keep checking actual progress against that schedule for compliance. When actual completion deviates much from the schedule (and this will most likely be on the slow side rather than on the fast side), it is time to determine what, if any, action should be taken.

As to the controls that should be built into programs, there is a countless list of things that could be included. We have all heard of the many strange things that computers have done by merely applying their specific programmed instructions to the data as furnished. Many of those absurd—and sometimes extremely harmful—results could have been avoided by the use of some simple program controls. On the other hand, it is easy to overdo things and attempt to set up controls that will check on every process that is to take place. At some point, that approach suffers from overkill. Some things aren't very likely to happen at all; some that are likely will be caught elsewhere; and others won't cause much trouble if and when they do occur.

A reasonable amount of time must be spent on determining what controls are built into the hardware or are part of the software supplied with the machine. There isn't much sense in putting in a program control if a situation has already been adequately provided for elsewhere. For example, while it may have been fashionable twenty years ago to have steps that checked on the arithmetic accuracy of the computer, most people today believe the computer has enough built-in checking features to make such a control unnecessary. Generally speaking, a risk assessment process should be used as a guide in how much checking to do.

Controls that can be built into computer programs are generally placed into three categories, namely, input controls, processing controls, and output controls. Although I will not use those categories directly, I will comment on the point of appropriate use.

There are two main restrictions on using the computer to check for errors. One is the ability of users, systems analysts, and programmers to develop the list of items to check for. The other is the willingness or competence of the programmer to write the applicable instructions. The computer time required to look for such errors is almost negligible in most cases.

Perhaps a presentation of statistics that show how bad computer results can be will convince all concerned that computer checking is not only desirable but mandatory. The lack of editing—or more correctly, the presence of errors not caught at all or caught much later than they should be—causes many problems. The outstanding ones are inaccurate reports, loss of confidence in the system when the errors are not caught at all, and the excess costs related to additional manual work and computer reruns when errors are caught and corrected. Generally, much of this extra cost would be unnecessary if the errors could be detected before a final report is run.

Reasonableness Checks

Just about every numerical field entering a computer has some reasonable lower and/or upper limit. It is a simple programming matter to test each field to see if the amount fits within the range. Note that in most cases the program can't determine if a value is *correct* (for instance, if an employee worked seven or eight hours on a particular day); it can only check to see if it is *reasonable* (for example, 40 hours per day would not pass the reasonableness test). To take another example, if a worker's hourly pay rate were inadvertently changed from $2.90 to $31.20 instead of $3.12, this mistake would have been caught by such a test. Even if $31.20 an hour were a valid pay rate for certain types of employees, this input error should be caught by a test of the increase as a percentage or by testing the compatibility between pay rate and job code. Often a field of data will have to be related to another field of data to determine its reasonableness. For example, a company doesn't often sell a high quantity of its highest-priced items (thus 150 Boeing 747s at $30 million each on one sale would be marked as suspicious).

It might be concluded that a good reasonableness test at the input stage would be a sufficient control. But that is not the case. Assume a good check has been made of both a worker's pay rate and the number of hours worked. Something could still be out of line regarding the worker's gross pay. This could come about because of faulty logic in the program. Thus here is a situation where a programmed control is checking not only on source input but also on programmer efforts.

Self-Checking Digit

This specific control can determine quite early in processing if a recording error has been made. Its value is that it catches mistakes earlier than many other controls. Another advantage is that there does not have to be any data file available to use it. As the name suggests, the account number of a transaction checks itself for validity.

Suppose there are only several hundred account numbers to assign. If no particular significance is involved in the account number, then a three-digit number will be sufficient. This code will provide up to 999 accounts. The use of a self-checking digit will append one more digit to the code, making it four digits long.

110 AUDITING THE DATA PROCESSING FUNCTION

This fourth self-checking digit is assigned by performing some mathematical process on the first three digits. An example would be to multiply the first digit by one, the second by two, and the third by three. Add the three products, eliminate any high-order digit in the total, and the units position becomes the self-checking digit. It would be a simple process for a computer to go through all possible codes, make the self-checking digit calculation, and print a list of account numbers ready to be assigned.

Here is an example using the above formula:

Three-Digit Code	Calculations	Sum	Self-Checking Digit	Complete Code
123	1 + 4 + 9	14	4	1234
197	1 + 18 + 21	40	0	1970
204	2 + 0 + 12	14	4	2044
581	5 + 16 + 3	24	4	5814
777	7 + 14 + 21	42	2	7772

Suppose you are assigning clock numbers to employees, and you decide to use the four-digit numbers as shown. Assume that John Doe is assigned the first code, number 1234. In the first week of work, he fills out his time sheet but makes a mistake when recording his clock number. He makes a transposition in the number, recording it as 1324. The time sheet is keypunched into a card or tape, key-verified, and then goes on to the computer. The first computer program that runs the data has a segment that verifies the self-checking digit. The computer reads all four digits, calculates a self-checking digit from the first three (in this case, 1 + 6 + 6 = 13 = 3), and compares that to the fourth. However, the calculated digit 3 does not equal the digit 4 that accompanied John's number, so the computer kicks the transaction out as being invalid.

While it is true that certain other controls might have caught the mistake at a later time, there is some value in catching mistakes as early as practical. (In Chapter 5 we will see a way to use the self-checking digit check even sooner than shown here.)

There are some obvious drawbacks to the use of the self-checking digit. It takes time to design and to use, since an extra character has to be recorded and entered into the computer. Also, it is in principle possible for a person to make a drastic recording error that nonetheless results in a valid code. But then, there is no other control that is perfect, either. Major uses of self-checking digits are for bank checking account numbers and credit card account numbers. Such codes occasionally have to be manually handled, and processing equipment could make a reading error. In either case any errors can be kicked out for inspection, possible correction, and reentry.

In a nationwide department store chain, the customer's credit card is automatically read by the sales clerk's terminal. The self-checking digit concept is used to make sure the terminal read the customer code correctly. Then when the sales clerk enters the account number of each item sold, an appropriate calculation is performed by the terminal to make sure that manual entry was correct.

Testing for Duplicates

In a situation where there is to be only one transaction per account, there should be a positive test to see that this restriction is met. Examples would be in a payroll system where there is to be only one time card per person or in a medical plan where there can be only one claim per illness. In a batch system, this can be easily checked by sorting the data to a specific sequence (say, alphabetically by last name or numerically by Social Security number) and checking adjacent records to see if they are duplicates. Of course, if it is necessary to process adjustments relating to a prior period, the system must be carefully set up so that it distinguishes legitimate adjustments and corrections from simple duplicates.

Testing for Excessive Activity

It is a simple matter to program the computer to count the number of occurrences of any type of transaction. Many categories of transactions should realistically occur only so often; any excess may not necessarily mean that something is wrong, but merely that the situation should be investigated.

Care must be taken to apply this concept properly. For example, an oil company sent 300 credit cards to an individual who had ordered 3 cards for his family. When questioned about permitting as many as 300 cards to be made out in one name, the company pointed out that it had an upward limit of 400. However, that great a quantity was set up to handle corporate accounts. The company's failure was in not having separate account codes for business and individual accounts and then a separate upper limit for each.

Another company was interested in the effectiveness with which it gave out credit cards. The computer center sorted all its credit card customers to street address within a ZIP code. It was quite surprised to find 17 different credit cards outstanding at a single-family dwelling. Several members of the family had each obtained multiple cards, which was contrary to the policy of the company.

Comparing Current Transactions to a File

Most data processing systems operate on the basis that transactions have to be processed against a file of related records. There is a simple reason for this: to keep the day-to-day recording of source data as scanty and efficient as possible, the system must be designed so that most of the data needed are kept in a computer-type file. In payroll, for example, the source data actually recorded might be restricted to name or clock number and hours worked. A payroll file can contain the dozens of other fields of data necessary to pay each employee. Thus a level of control can be gained by merely comparing the current detail transactions to the file. By carefully noting in the file those employees who have been terminated, this check would identify current pay transactions that were not valid. Furthermore, the system could be set up to accept overtime work only if the file had been previously set up to authorize it. Of course, you have to assess whether you can afford to wait that long to find errors or if you should set up some controls that can be made to work earlier in the system.

Sequence Checking

The typical computer run still operates on the basis that data are processed in a meaningful sequence, such as by clock number in payroll, vendor number in accounts payable, or part number in inventory control. The computer itself is used to put the data into sequence, and various programs contain the steps to make sure the sequence is maintained. Data out of sequence not only cause a problem for any person who has to handle the output but also make it difficult to check for duplicate transactions.

Record Counts

In most applications, the number of records handled is a vital piece of information. There may be a predetermined number of records to balance to (such as the number of people to be paid), or the program may count the transactions and the number is to be made available to and used in a later process.

The Batch Total

A batch total is a control that involves manually getting a total of a numerical field before data are entered in the computer. The computer calculates a total of the same field of data. The two totals are then tested to see if they are equal. If they are, each individual transaction was probably entered into the computer correctly; if not, an error was made and must be found and corrected.

As an example, accounting clerks ordinarily calculate a total of the money collected from customers; the total of the individual credits to accounts-receivable records should equal that predetermined total. Also, the total of accounts receivable before payments minus total cash received should equal the total of accounts receivable after processing.

It is one thing to use the batch total concept and yet another to use it correctly. The computer could presumably be employed in two different ways in dealing with the totals:

114 AUDITING THE DATA PROCESSING FUNCTION

1. Merely have the computer print out the relevant numbers at the end of the run. Provide for a person to visually review the numbers and compare them to the predetermined values. If the totals don't agree, the person is to take a specified action.
2. Make up control cards that contain the predetermined values. Feed them into the computer at the very beginning or end of the run. Have the computer develop the totals during the processing run. At the end of the run, the

Figure 8. Two methods of checking input codes.

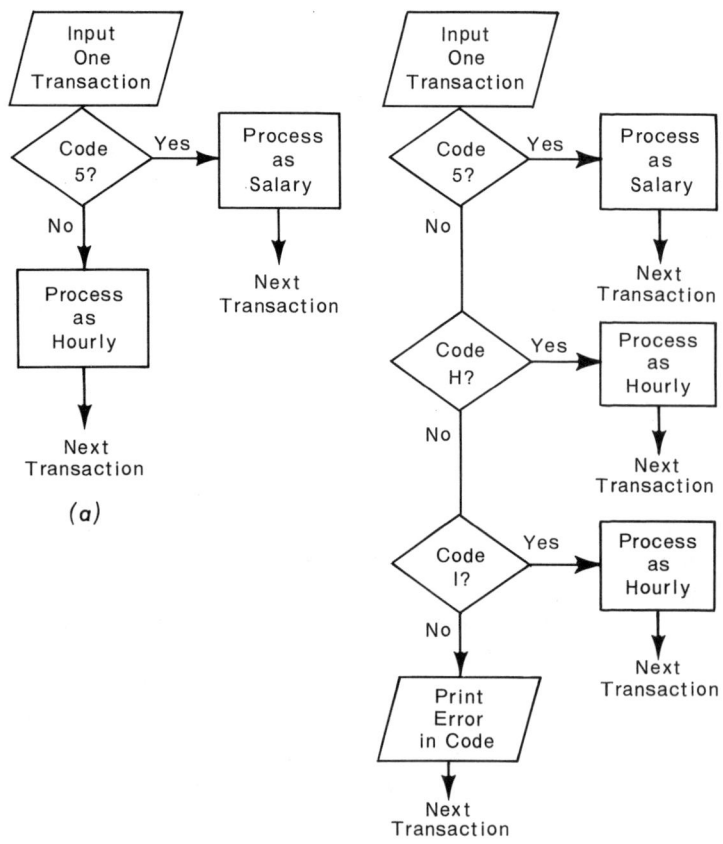

computer program will compare the numbers generated during the run to the predetermined totals. The program will then indicate if the totals balance or not.

In the first case, the system is subject to the integrity of the person doing the checking. Management may or may not want the checking to be done that way. A sound reason for not doing it that way is that here is a form of drudgery that can be taken from a person and given to the computer. In the second case, the computer can be programmed to prevent further processing until some positive action is taken as a follow-up to an out-of-balance condition.

Editing Procedures

The computer can be programmed to look for the presence or absence of any condition. Examples are:

○ Missing fields in a record. (The last line of an address should have a city, a state, and a ZIP code.)
○ Missing characters (blanks) within a field. (A Social Security number must contain nine digits; there cannot be any internal blank positions.)
○ Impermissible characters in a field. A field may be restricted to all numeric (a clock number) or all alphabetic (a state name), or it may permit a mixture of characters.
○ An unreasonable numerical value, either less or more than a specific predetermined amount. (For example, a quantity may not be allowed to be a negative number.) However, watch for adjustments that could cause something like negative hours worked. The system may have to be set up so that such unusual transactions as negative hours worked can enter only as adjustments, which would then have their own method of authorization, input source forms, and extra control features.
○ Specific data values or codes. Although this requirement can cause a great deal of programming effort in cases where there are many values or codes to check, the payoff can be handsome. Please refer to the program flowchart in Figure 8. Version (*a*) accepts any code other than 5 as an

hourly person. Version (b) tests for the presence of each valid code; it does not assume a code is one thing just because it is not another. Instead, it kicks out any transactions that do not have a valid code. (Note, however, that this type of test is not foolproof; in particular, it can't determine if a valid code is being *used* correctly.)
- A combination check. A customer which is a city, and therefore not subject to a sales tax, should not have a sales tax percentage.

What to do about editing errors once they have been detected is a different problem. In most cases you can't afford to halt the computer upon detection, since it would take an unreasonable amount of time for the operator to find out what the correction should be. Secondly, you probably don't want the computer operator to make the correction anyway.

The best approach is to program the computer to print an error message that conveniently identifies the error and have it just keep moving along. Figure 9 shows several ways to do this, with the last alternative being the preferred style. The first two styles both require too much work on the part of the person working with the edit run printout.

The preceding discussion on handling errors refers to a batch-type system. If the data recording is to be on-line, it is desirable to have on-line editing programs and relevant data files immediately available to the computer. In this way, all the editing techniques listed above can be employed. A message can immediately be sent back to the person entering the data with a clear indication as to what is wrong. Hopefully the person can correct the error right away through a reentry, and the editing program can look at it again, using the same procedures as before.

If the on-line editing process has appropriate files available, then even more can be done. Suppose that in a production system the computer has a file of open job numbers. Editing can reject attempted charges to jobs that aren't open. Similarly, in a purchase order and receiving system, the computer can reject an unreasonable quantity or an attempt to report a receipt for an item that hadn't been ordered.

Figure 9. Three styles of identifying editing errors.

SIMPLE FLAGGING BY ASTERISK

Account No.	Amount
187*	$50.00
194	$12.00*
382*	$853.00*

ERROR CODES:

Account No.	Amount	Error Code
187	$50.00	A
194	$12.00	P
382	$853.00	AB

EXPLICIT ERROR MESSAGES

Account No.	Error Message	Amount	Error Message
187	Invalid Account	$50.00	
194		$12.00	Too small
382	Invalid Account	$853.00	Too large

Built-in Hardware Controls

In designing a control system it is helpful to know what has already been provided by the computer manufacturer.

In recent years we have come to expect, and rightly so, that computers and their related hardware devices are designed in such a way that they either do not make mistakes or at least correct any mistake made and continue on or stop if a mistake was made that couldn't automatically be corrected.

The types of built-in features include, but are not limited to:

Parity check. This is an electronic feature that makes sure the machine is not adding or dropping electronic bits; if it were, that would have the effect of altering data. For example, if a bit were dropped, an alphabetic Z might be converted to a numeric *1*. This test works on reading and writing such media as tapes and discs, and it controls all internal movement of data in the CPU.

Validity check. A punched card does not provide for parity; instead, there are only so many valid combinations of holes that can exist in a punched card column. The validity check rejects any card with invalid combinations.

Dual read. Some reading devices read all input twice and automatically compare the results to make sure no reading mistake was made.

A read after a write. When a computer records onto a tape or a disc, it immediately reads what it just wrote and compares it to what it was supposed to write.

Overflow. If a calculated value is too large for the area reserved for it by the programmer, the computer makes a signal available pointing that out. A program step must test for presence of such a signal and do something about it; otherwise, the excess data that don't fit will be lost.

Programmers need to become intimately familiar with these controls and what they do. Auditors, too, need to learn about them to make sure maximum value is gained from their use.

The Best Control?

One of the controls that can provide the most effective results and yet be cheap is that afforded by responsible, motivated employees. Provide some encouragement here, and you will be surprised how much of a return you can get.

Consider the case of a wholesale grocer who tried to deliver a truckload of peas to a corner grocery, on the basis of a computerized shipping order. Certainly the people who loaded the truck knew that order was wrong, but something had happened to cause them to give up the use of common sense. As another example illustrating this point, I have heard often that keypunch personnel are to keypunch what they see, without exception. This means that they will pass on some input they know to be wrong, with the idea that it is someone else's problem. My own feeling is that I want keypunch personnel who become familiar enough with the source data and care enough to reject data with obvious errors. However, they should not be authorized to correct errors in source data.

In sum, we need more of an effort to get people concerned about the impact of their actions on the total organization. This can be done partially by instituting training programs that teach employees how the various segments of the business fit together to form a unity. Reasonable incentives—not necessarily monetary—for those who do a good job may also be effective. Finally, a decent human relations program can go a long way toward making people care about what happens to their organization.

AUDITING THE PROGRAM DEVELOPMENT PHASE

One approach an auditor might take is to review programs as they are being prepared so as to ensure their adequacy prior to implementation. Alternatively, the review could wait until the programs have been installed and have begun to produce results on a regular day-to-day basis. A problem with the former approach is that it may be difficult to pull all the pieces of the system together to perform an effective review so early in the game. A problem with the latter approach is that by the time programs are installed, it might become difficult to make changes.

Generalized Audit Software

This represents a program or a set of programs written specifically for audit purposes. All large CPA firms have had such packages written for their specific needs. Furthermore, there are numerous software firms offering general-purpose audit packages for sale. These are typically bought by smaller CPA firms and internal auditors.

A package of generalized audit software represents a tremendous investment that few users could afford. Hence the development of this auditing tool is usually restricted to organizations that have the means to spread the cost over many users.

The term *generalized* is appropriate for these programs because the software is not designed to relate to a specific application. It can be made to work on payroll as well as on accounts payable. Of course, this means it has its limits, as anything "generalized" always does.

Most of these packages have the following capabilities, among others:

Performing various arithmetic functions, such as totaling, cross-footing, and recalculating any previously performed steps.

Selecting sample transactions on almost any logical basis desired.

Preparing reports in many different formats, having selected and sorted the proper records according to the specifications provided by the auditor.

Comparing the records in one file with those in another file.

Preparing confirmation forms on such applications as accounts payable and accounts receivable.

While advertising literature for generalized audit software may suggest that all an auditor needs to do to use the package is to fill out a simple specification form, experience shows that the matter is a little more involved than that. Generally, the auditor must have a basic knowledge of EDP operations and the common terms used in that field. In addition, the auditor should have anywhere from two to five days of solid training in the use of the package.

As mentioned before, a generalized set of programs must try to be all things to all people. Hence it often falls short of containing a specific feature that is desired. Either that feature must be provided by modifying the program, or one may have to give up trying to perform certain desirable functions.

The Test Data Method

In the test data method, the auditor makes up some sample transactions and processes those data with the client's production program. In order to do a good job here, the auditor obviously needs to know the application well. Also, some creativity is needed to come up with sample data that are representative of what can happen in day-to-day transactions. For example, in payroll you would want to enter some unusual pay rates and abnormal hours worked; also, there should be data that would create a negative net pay for a person. In inventory control, there should be a transaction for a nonexistent part number and an inventory withdrawal that would create a negative inventory balance for an item.

An alternative would be to carefully observe what production programs do to live data. The main problem with that method, apart from the quantity of data required, is that one never really knows what the computer would do with a situation that happened to be missing from the live data. Thus, many auditors prefer to make a positive test using made-up data.

Parallel Simulation

This process is also called reprocessing. The client's data are first processed with the client's program. Using a specially prepared program, the data are then processed again, and the results of the reprocessing are compared to the client's original results. Thus the auditor gets a good feel for how well the production program works.

This method has the apparent disadvantage of requiring all the time necessary to write a program that copies the steps contained in the production program. However, many programming short cuts can be taken by directly providing for only major situations and letting the others fall out as exceptions. In many cases, the number of such exceptions will be few and pose no serious problem.

Also, there is the problem of who will write the program.

Many auditors do not have the expertise required and must look elsewhere for help. Engaging the services of a programmer is acceptable as long as sufficient control is maintained to ensure that the program is written exactly to the auditor's specifications.

Parallel simulation is the auditing technique that seems to hold the most promise for detecting programmed fraud. Thus its use is bound to increase significantly. However, a parallel simulation program needs to be used a number of times in order to justify its cost of preparation. As generalized audit software programs become more flexible in use, the need to write specific programs should decline.

Reviewing Programs

At one time it was proposed that auditors simply review production programs to make sure they were doing the job right. However, this has never become a popular method, mainly because many auditors lacked the technical expertise required and because it is difficult and time-consuming to try to follow another person's program.

With the increasing programming knowledge of the typical auditor and new programming techniques that more carefully structure the writing of programs so they are easier to follow by others, this method may fulfill its promise of becoming quite appropriate and therefore popular. My personal prediction is that its use will increase significantly.

Accuracy

Considering that a computer program has to do so many different things and may require thousands of steps to do them all, it is no wonder that programming errors are so easily made. However, there are many things a programmer can do to help develop some level of accuracy. The first is to demand a clear-cut problem definition from the systems analyst. Hopefully the systems standards call for the applicable user to have officially indicated full agreement with the system as it is being developed. In those cases where the systems analyst is also the programmer, the potential for a misunderstanding among data processing specialists will evidently be reduced if not eliminated.

Since flowcharts can be difficult for some people to understand, it may not help much for a programmer to show flowcharts to a user to make sure the program is on the right track. Instead, the use of a print layout form should be an easy medium to use for that purpose. A print layout form is used to indicate exactly what data the computer is to print and exactly where on the printed page they are to appear. Have the programmer take a couple of sample transactions and show the user what processing would take place. The parties should soon know if the processing logic is all right or not.

Once an auditor is on the scene reviewing the programmer's efforts—whether before or after the programs are put into production—the first thing to do is to see if the adopted programming standards have been followed. Of particular interest is a check to see if there has been reasonable communication with the user. Where it is clear that the programmer has not done a good job in those respects, the auditor must decide how to handle the situation, in particular, whether to raise this as a personnel issue. Management may want to be informed about such problems and who caused them. Whereas an external auditor is most likely to report the person, perhaps an internal auditor would first try to persuade the programmer to comply with the standards.

The auditor may choose to operate somewhat like a user, waiting to get some computer output and then checking it for accuracy. Several of the techniques described in the previous section may also be used. In this connection, it must be emphasized that although both test decks and parallel simulation are a check on accuracy, they serve different purposes. Test decks are used mainly to check if a given *program* is adequate. This is mostly a test of *compliance*—were certain essential things done, and how? By contrast, parallel simulation is mainly a test for *substance*—that is, it checks the correctness of the *results* produced by a program from its data.

When a financial auditor is called upon to attest that total accounts receivable, for example, are a reasonable amount, the auditor is concerned about a substantive test. However, if a compliance test shows that good procedures have been used in processing the data, then the extent of any substantive tests can be reduced.

Efficiency

It is hard to determine efficiency of the program development function for two reasons. First, it is difficult to estimate how long it should take to write a program. Second, a programmer necessarily spends a good deal of time thinking and even gazing out a window; thus even if you were there to observe the person, it would be difficult to determine if he or she is "working."

Since two programs are rarely very similar, and since you can hardly have two programmers do the same job just to determine who was more "efficient," much information that would be nice to have is difficult to get.

One data processing manager I know has developed a method that works well for him. Since he is quite familiar with all the programs that have to be written in his shop, he has a programmer make a time estimate for an upcoming job. Then the job specifications are given to an outside software house to obtain a quote from them. If that quote is much better, he often contracts for the job with the software house. However, he is always careful to make sure the quote hasn't been kept low by the outside house merely to get the job.

A side benefit of this procedure is that job specifications coming from his systems group are more complete than ever before. This is because a software house isn't likely to sign a fixed-price contract for something it doesn't understand. By contrast, internal programmers are not always so careful to get potential trouble spots cleared up before they start writing programs.

The second aspect of the efficiency problem—how efficiently programs run—is not as critical as it once was. In prior years, internal computer capacity was small and expensive. Programmers therefore had to go out of their way to reduce the number of instructions used. Now, with personnel tending to be a bigger cost factor than hardware, an extra one hundred or so instructions or a "slow" internal computer process is not viewed as such a serious matter.

Some organizations have obtained *software monitors* to check on certain features used in programs. A software monitor is a special program that checks for such things as instructions that are present but are never executed during the running of a job and instructions that are executed more often than they need to be. Software monitors are available from computer manufacturers and software houses.

Fraud

The statistics on computer crime and fraud indicate that a number of programmers have defrauded their employers through the use of improper steps in computer programs. These recorded frauds include the following examples:

> Taking extra pay either by issuing a check larger than authorized or by issuing an extra check. Note that various system controls should catch the latter type of fraud.
> "Stealing" from someone else, for example, by reducing every employee's "taxes withheld" by $1 and placing the total on the programmer's own W-2. There have been cases of rounding transactions whereby the programmer's personal account receives all the third or fourth decimal portions from all other accounts.
> Crediting a customer's account receivable for money not actually received.
> Writing out accounts-payable checks for phony purchases.

Many organizations go to great lengths to prevent computer programmers from entering the computer room. Note, however, that the programmer doesn't have to go near the computer to pull off any of the four styles above. Essentially all the programmer needs to do is write and submit programs. If other controls aren't in place and working, he can then sit back and reap the benefits.

One of the effective approaches to control fraud, regardless of the method used by the crook, is to investigate the slightest irregularity to see if there is a pattern. If an account is off by a dollar or so, don't blindly accept the excuse that it is a "rounding error." Track it down fully and see if there are others similar to it. If some type of pattern emerges, you may be on the way to catching the thief.

Some organizations investigate their programmers both before and periodically during employment. For example, an employee who is heavily in debt or who has developed unusually heavy spending habits may be considered to be a threat. Other practices are to rotate programmers among applications, to use a certain separation of duties, and to bond programmers.

Security

Hopefully the programming situation has not deteriorated to the point where you have to search all programmers on the way out to make sure they aren't taking a vital program to an unauthorized outsider. Usually, security is more concerned with ensuring that program plans and listings can't be easily picked up by outsiders. Relevant controls are the provision of adequate lockable filing space and the use of shredders to destroy any paper that is no longer needed. Magnetic tapes and disc packs can be either erased or damaged beyond use prior to being discarded.

If the system is of the type that can be accessed from a terminal, then a careful process of issuing and controlling account numbers is called for. Account numbers should be changed often, and the computer should keep a record of all accesses. An auditor may test this phase of security by simply looking around terminals and telephones for account numbers that might have been placed there openly for the user's convenience.

Perhaps a more basic security concern is to establish internal methods to prevent programs from becoming erased. These methods include the proper use of file protect rings and internal labels and establishment of an effective library system. The auditor can effectively determine through physical observation how well all these methods work. Also, there should be a system of duplicate programs to facilitate recovery.

Overall Effectiveness

This can best be checked by talking with customers; they will generally let you know quickly if programs do the right things. Also, if computer output is obviously dog-eared from use, that is a sign that the programs produce adequate results. Another method is to find out from users how they actually use the output. Ordinarily they should have no reason to cover up for a poor job in program development.

5

Raw Data Generation and Data Conversion

Raw data generation and data conversion are the two areas of an EDP system whose day-to-day operation involves by far the greatest number of people and man-hours. Furthermore, not only are the people responsible for raw data generation not under the control of the EDP department, they also represent a rather diverse group. Many of them have no concept of where they fit in the overall picture, and unfortunately some of them could hardly care less. The input area represents the major potential bottleneck in day-to-day operations, since the computer center cannot start any useful work until the raw data have been generated and converted to a format that the computer can handle.

Although the use of on-line input alleviates some of these problems, many of them remain.

GOALS

The goal of raw data generation and data conversion is to provide accurate and relevant source data for the computer in a timely and cost-effective fashion. There are two groups of people who are doing this work: those in source departments who create the data, and those who convert it to computer-readable form. However, there is some dependency on others as well. Systems analysts have to see that the right source data are created. There are those concerned with moving the data to the computer center, whether they be internal messengers, the U.S. Postal Service, or a telephone company. Computer programmers also come into play, since it is necessary to write programs that will either validate data or kick out invalid data for manual review.

STANDARDS

With so much of the success of a system depending on so many people as it is in data generation and conversion, good standards are probably needed more in these areas than in any others. The more critical ones include:
 1. Develop concise and meaningful source data coding structures that make coding simple and that help avoid errors. For example, use *F* and *M,* respectively, to denote male and female, instead of assigning codes such as *1* and *2*. Provide for checkmarks instead of requiring that specific characters be entered.
 2. Pay close attention to forms design. Make sure no unnecessary data are requested on any form and that all forms are clear and easy to use so as to avoid recording errors.
 3. Develop reasonable cutoff points to signify the end of one accounting period and the beginning of the next.
 4. Make sure people in source departments spend only a minor part of their time on paperwork. (Salespersons should spend most of their time selling, not filling out forms.)
 5. Establish reasonable minimum key-stroking speeds for all applications, but keep in mind any factors that would justify variations in speed.
 6. Use reasonable control procedures over source generation steps, making sure to check the non-EDP parts just as

much as the others. Maintain these controls as close to the source as possible. It is cheaper and easier to make corrections at the front end.

7. Be certain to determine what kinds of errors happen most often, then develop appropriate controls and correction procedures specifically for those errors.

8. Develop error statistics as to the type of error and who or what caused each. While auditors may not have the authority to remove ineffective workers, the data should be available so the proper level of management can do so.

9. In those cases where on-line entry is to be used, the only justification for it to replace traditional batch entry is for cost-benefit reasons. No value should be placed upon intangibles, such as faster service from on-line entry, unless savings can be proved to be realistic. Furthermore, it must be shown that on-line entry methods can be reasonably controlled as to accuracy, or they should not be adopted. (Perhaps this point is really one of system development, but it is important to consider it here.)

10. When considering changes in data generation and conversion, be careful to properly evaluate the present investments in both employee training and capital equipment. For instance, management may not wish to throw away the investment in keypunch machines.

TRANSACTION AUTHORIZATION

It is important to make sure that only properly authorized transactions get into the work flow. The consequences of receiving and perhaps processing some unauthorized transactions are quite obvious.

The starting point is to determine who is authorized to create and/or approve transactions. This may be clear-cut in some cases and quite difficult to determine in others. For each application, it should be possible to draw up a list showing who is authorized; by definition, all others are excluded. There may be some applications in which the authority of people at certain levels is granted for certain amounts, such as for pay raises or the purchase of fixed assets. But such systems should have some strength in them to discourage working around the rules. For example, if management has issued a mandate that supervisors are not authorized to buy more than $1,000 of fixed assets, then the system should be set up to come down on any supervisor who tries to buy $1,200 worth by breaking such a purchase up into two transactions of $600 each.

Proper authorization can often be accomplished by careful attention to forms control. The forms are often held in strict custody, where they are difficult for just anyone to obtain. And in some systems those forms, when completed, have to be delivered in special envelopes. For example, in a state that requires physical examinations for people applying for driver's licenses, the form recording the results of the examination must be received at the State License Bureau in a special envelope.

The use of prenumbered forms, special custody of forms, and insistence on certain signatures all help to protect against unauthorized transactions. (Countersignatures may also be of value.) Unfortunately, many systems are designed (or operated) so ridiculously that a signature doesn't mean anything; it is thoughtlessly applied, often by a delegate, through the use of a rubber stamp, printed by the computer, or even placed on the form by the printer at the time the form is produced.

Of course, the most ingeniously designed and carefully controlled form is worthless if a transaction can get punched into a card for entry to the computer, since it is difficult to program the computer to find out if an input card was punched from a valid form or if it was just punched according to the desire of an operator. One control is to require a coding structure known only to a few people. Another control is to count the source forms used by authorized people and to compare that count to the number received by the computer.

There will be situations where a computer program will actually "authorize" a transaction. For example, in inventory control the computer might place an order to obtain more of an item when a predetermined order point has been reached. It is most desirable to have system segments of this type, because they can free people of much routine paperwork. The number of places where something can go wrong is greatly reduced, and system and program controls can be applied to make the process secure.

Except for situations of this type, which are under heavy program control, people who work in the computer center should not be authorized to create any transactions. They are typically meant to be service people whose function is to process the transactions created by others. You may even want to limit the ability of computer center people to correct transactions when errors are found, except under rather strict circumstances.

It is a normal rule of internal control that people who have custody of assets cannot be allowed to initiate transactions in the areas in which they serve. For instance, people who work in the storeroom should not be permitted to prepare requisitions that authorize inventory withdrawals. Or people who handle accounts-receivable records should not be allowed to write off any accounts receivable that are created by bad debt situations.

Some accounts-payable systems obviously need to be strengthened with regard to the "bills" they pay. In 1977 and later many companies were plagued by the receipt of what appeared to be a bill for some service to be provided in the future, typically some form of advertising. In most cases, the fine print at the bottom of the form merely said that by paying the bill, the company would get its name printed in a future advertising brochure—that is, its name and address would appear in the brochure, but there would be no advertising copy along with it. Evidently, the service to be obtained by paying the bill was worthless. Yet many businesses routinely paid these "bills" because they looked so authentic. One reason for this no doubt was that the bills offered an attractive discount for payment within ten days. The success of this scheme suggests that many accounts-payable systems need to improve their matching of services ordered with services received before making payments.

Perhaps more auditing attention should be paid to adjusting

entries (of the error correction type) and to the creation of new master records. For one thing, the number of error corrections is a serious issue because of the cost involved, and by studying them in detail, it may be possible to reduce them. Also, both areas are prone to fraudulent manipulation. Thus you can't put your control efforts only on the routine day-to-day transactions. A typical control is to require one or more levels of approval for all entries other than the routine type. Such entries should be initiated by a person, not by a computer program. (Note that there are some transactions in which computer initiation is acceptable, such as ordering more inventory at the proper time.)

One way for an auditor to test the authorization system is to try to process a transaction himself. In auditing a certain payroll system, for example, an auditor learned a reasonable amount about how the system worked. The hardware used was a computer with various kinds of secondary storage, a terminal for keyboard input, and a line printer for output. The auditor entered the name of Mickey Mouse as a new employee along with a certain number of days worked. Sure enough, as he expected, the line printer prepared a paycheck in the name of Mickey Mouse. The auditor's suggestions for improvement were that the authorization for a new employee should come from one place and the requests to pay employees from another. This dual authorization process imposed an almost automatic control instead of leaving the system to the whims of one person at one terminal.

PROCEDURES

The procedures involved in source data generation tend to be either of two major types:

1. Transactions occur (A) and are recorded on sheets of paper (B), which are collected into batches and moved to the computer center (C). There the data are keyed onto either cards, tape, or disc (D). A verification of the keying operation takes place (E) before the data go to the computer. The data enter the computer and are edited by a program (F). Erroneous

data are kicked out and sent back to a prior point for correction (G).

2. In an on-line entry mode, many of the processes mentioned above either occur differently or not at all. There may be no recording on paper (B). While there may or may not be batching, movement is over a telephone line. Keying at the job site replaces key-stroking at the computer center (D). Processes F and G are quite similar. The on-line editing replaces the separate verification step.

Perhaps there is a tendency to think of a system as operating in a much more confined way than it realistically can. For example, many introductory data processing texts depict a payroll system as operating in the simple manner shown in either segment of Figure 10. Each of these system flowcharts is

Figure 10. System flowcharts that inadequately portray the payroll process.

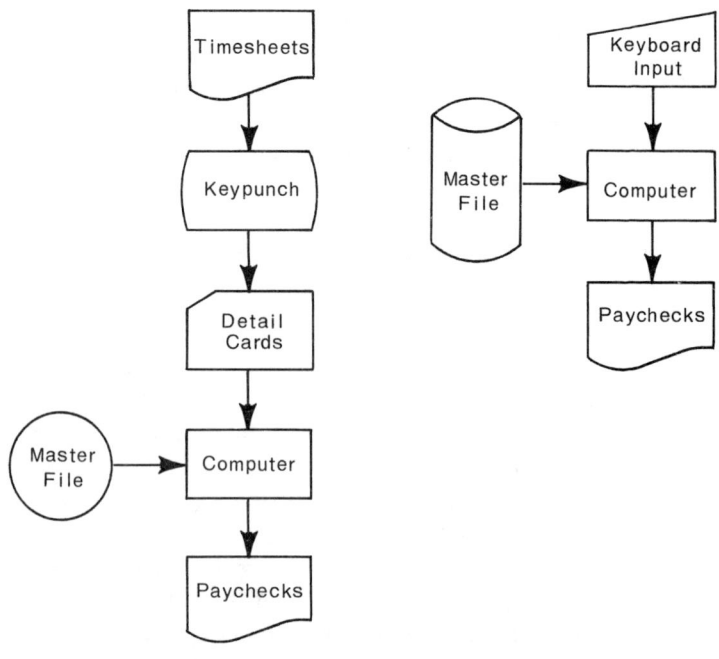

somewhat misleading, however, because systems don't tend to work that simply.

In real-life systems, lots of things can go wrong. Many errors occur all along the way. Examples are source documents with fields containing too many characters; the use of words or terms instead of the required codes; and transaction amounts far beyond the bounds of the system. Data arrive late, and reruns are necessary. Thus there is much more of a flow of data involved with more interactions and disciplined repetition of certain phases before the data are correct or complete enough to finish processing. A real deficiency of classroom instruction is the inability to recognize how great the error problem is and how great the total volume of data to be processed can get. Furthermore, classroom exercises too often have a pat answer that balances out more nicely than reality does.

A major procedural issue is what to do to protect against the loss of documents in the process of sending them to the computer center. There are all kinds of ways to approach this problem. One is to do nothing, hoping that it isn't important, that it won't happen, or that it will be self-correcting (someone will let you know about it). Another way is to copy everything into a log; this method is not only costly but also subject to writing errors. Another alternative is to create all transactions in multiple copies and retain one copy at or near the source.

The very nature of a batch system is to collect so many transactions as a group. This group may be all the time sheets of a department for an hour, day, week, or some other span of time, or it might be an approximate number of transactions. I once set up a system with the instruction that a batch was to be "about 50 transactions." When I later checked to see how things were going, I found the people counting out exactly 50 transactions per batch. We reviewed the purpose of the batching process; the people then noted the general height of a card deck representing 50 transactions and soon found it was about one finger. Using this rough measure, we found the actual batch size varied generally between 40 and 60, and it worked just fine.

Regardless of the batch size that is chosen, there is the question of when and how often to submit data from the source area to EDP. Of course you could send one whole period's transactions at once, such as the week's time cards. But if, for example, in a payroll system there are daily job cards that can stand alone, there is much merit in transmitting them more often than weekly. If that is done, perhaps the EDP center can begin some work on the data before all the transactions bunch up and create a bottleneck.

One method that can be used to significantly reduce effort in the input area is the use of a turnaround document. This form is either a punched card or a sheet of paper that is output from the computer in one step, is sent to another department to serve a specific purpose (which could include adding some new data to it), and then is returned to the computer later as input. An example is the punched card many telephone companies send along to customers with the usual invoice. The customer is asked to return the card with the payment. When this is done, it reduces much of the key-stroking otherwise required at the telephone company in order to inform the computer who paid how much, since the card already contains the account number and hopefully the exact amount that the customer is paying. If the customer does not pay the exact amount owed, then a new card must be prepared based upon the customer payment. Certainly an EDP auditor would want to be able to recommend the use of turnaround documents where a client was using a more costly or less effective method of creating computer input.

All the people who design input forms should have to work on the firing line for a while with customers lined up waiting for service. This "control" would probably lead to greatly improved forms.

In an interesting case, a new input form was designed. It essentially asked for much more data than the previous form did. In fact, much of the new information requested was fixed and already available in the computer files. Since so much more raw data were requested, the physical size of the input form had to be expanded. This meant that the new form didn't fit in a standard-size typewriter, so people who used to type on the form now had to prepare the source data by hand. Also, the new forms were so large that even those that could be prepared on a typewriter couldn't be scanned at the computer center because they wouldn't fit in a scanner. Therefore, all source data had to be keypunched, and the conversion of source data soon degenerated to a backlog of several months.

The possibilities of mark sensing should also be investigated. One advantage to be gained is that the data need to be handled only once by the person most familiar with those data. This eliminates the need for disinterested people such as keypunch and verifier operators to become involved, and it avoids the tremendous costs and bottlenecks associated with those operations.

Of course you can apply mark sensing only in those cases where it has a good chance of success. Since mark sensing replaces the traditional placement of source data on a preprinted form, its original recording is actually performed by the person who creates the transaction. It will take a careful study to determine if that person can do the job as accurately by mark sensing as by writing it down on a source document form. Other considerations are the requirements of an environment consistent with such recording (the absence of rain or oil which make such documents unreadable) and enough of a volume to make automatic reading equipment economical.

Error Correction

While serving as a data processing manager, I once entered the computer room to see an operator removing a punched card from a deck, throwing it away, and replacing it with another. He said he was merely correcting an error in the source data. But while the computer detail and the resulting totals may now have been "correct," there was no way to reconcile subsequent computer runs back to the first edit run nor to the original source data.

To resolve that issue we quickly adopted a worthwhile standard: henceforth all errors other than those of the simple keypunching type would be corrected by making a credit equal to the original error and entering a new transaction card for the proper transaction. This situation created the need for another change. In those systems where a count of the number of records was necessary, we had to be careful to treat the above situation as a single transaction and not three, since there would now be three records for such an item. The new system also called for changes in the source document, since it previously had not contained a convenient way to show that a transaction was to be treated as a credit, that is, to back it out.

Data Retention

It seems to me there is more misinformation on retention requirements than on any other topic. Usually people's opinion as to how long data must be kept is on the high rather than the low side. To put it another way, people are usually overprotective of data.

The three factors relevant here are laws, company policy, and regular operating purposes. These may or may not conflict considerably with each other. In any event, legal requirements ordinarily are the controlling feature. However, an organization should investigate the possibilities of working out special arrangements. The IRS is in principle willing to make such arrangements, as evidenced by its Revenue Ruling 71-20. That ruling provides for the taxpayer to negotiate specific retention procedures with the local office of the IRS.

It is encouraging to note that most careful studies show that regular operating procedures do not require so much historical data as one is inclined to believe. It appears that much data are retained to serve only audit purposes; the obvious solution is to encourage more timely audits so the throw-away campaign can begin sooner. In any event, data retention is an issue that should really be resolved at an early point in time—ideally when the system is developed.

DOCUMENTATION

The bulk of the documentation in the areas of data generation and conversion will be procedure manuals describing the steps to be performed and samples of the various forms that will be encountered. With respect to raw data generation, the documentation might consist of:

> Instructions as to how to fill out each input form. This may include any special routing of the form within or among departments. Instructions may be on separate sheets or on the forms themselves.
> Samples of the blank forms and of completed forms.
> Any instructions for control procedures such as batching and simple totaling. Also included may be the steps needed to send the completed input forms to the data conversion center.

The data conversion documentation may include the following items:

> Samples of the completed forms that conversion personnel are to receive.
> The format in which the computer record will be prepared, that is, a layout of the punched card or the tape or disc that will result.
> The instructions necessary to convert the data, including the steps to follow when conversion errors or other obvious errors are detected.
> The steps to follow in moving the completed data along to the next phase.
> Time standards for each job. This may be appropriate if there is a high volume of conversion work, and it generally is a necessity when the workers are on an incentive-pay program.

Since all the documentation mentioned above applies to so many people and also is of the type that can be prepared by people other than those who have to do the day-to-day work of recording and conversion, there will be a certain amount of natural pressure to keep it up to date. This is not so likely to happen with system and programming documentation, since the latter types largely must be prepared by the people performing the function, and those people often have a way of avoiding documentation unless they are pushed into it.

CONTROLS

Control in raw data generation must be built in from the very beginning. The obvious starting point is a clear determination of exactly what input data are needed, given the objectives of each application. Next, it should be determined how much of this information can be obtained by nonclerical means, that is, through automatic generation by the computer; then the remainder must be generated by people.

Probably the most important controls in the source departments are good employee selection methods; proper training; well-documented, clear procedures; and adequate supervision. Unfortunately, this segment of the operation is often overlooked by EDP managers, probably because much of it occurs outside the walls of the computer center. But an abundance of work is done here. There are many opportunities for control, and the needs for auditing are tremendous.

A major question is whether there is a way to tell if a person has made an error in recording a transaction. The answer is yes. There are a few ways that can be used effectively. With respect to the recording of the identification part of a transaction, the use of a self-checking digit is a major help. (This control was described in the preceding chapter.) Since the checking itself is done either by the keypunch machine or when the data enter the computer, it is not obvious to the person doing the original recording that an error has been made; an error caught by either checking process is merely

RAW DATA GENERATION AND DATA CONVERSION 141

kicked out without any display of information indicating exactly what is wrong.

It could be argued that the self-checking digit feature is not really needed, since the source data could be compared to valid master records, after entering the computer, to determine if an invalid transaction has occurred. While that statement is largely true, there is great value to finding out about such errors sooner rather than later. Furthermore, much of the value of an on-line system comes from compressing the amount of time elapsed between the creation of a transaction and checking it. The self-checking digit provides for that checking when all information about the transaction is still readily available to the person responsible for it.

Another control is the use of redundant information. For example, when recording an inventory transaction, one might record the applicable part number and the first three characters of the part description. The computer later matches the input with a master file to see if the two parts of the identification are compatible. Major problems with this method are the inconvenience of obtaining both fields of data and the time required in recording and keypunching the extra characters. The computer checking part should not be that much of an added chore.

Even when the redundancy concept is not used, the computer may still help because it can compare current transactions with a master file to see if all items are valid. For example, the computer can kick out any payroll transactions for any clock numbers of people not on the master payroll file. Similarly, it can reject a receiving report on a part number for which there is no outstanding purchase order. Unfortunately, a problem arises here where a transaction occurs for an identification code that is valid but happens to be the wrong one.

Computer programs can be set up as a means of anticipating input. This is especiallly useful in alerting people that a transaction is to occur but hasn't yet. Its use is obvious in payroll data for people who have master records, since everyone who has a master record should be turning in current pay data. Similarly, an open purchase order is expected to have a receiving report at a relevant time.

Other tasks for which the computer can be used effectively are to report on suspense file items that have not yet been cleared out or to list all purchase orders that haven't had any receipt of material within a reasonable time after such receipt was expected.

Another control that can and should be computerized is a check for two transactions against an account number when in fact only one is valid, such as in payroll. As to whether the amount portion of a transaction is all right or not, the people doing the recording represent the first line of defense; the problem is whether they care.

In most cases, it is up to a later editing program to check if quantities are reasonable. Unfortunately, there is little the computer can do to determine if an amount is *correct;* a program can only look to see if it is reasonable, given certain criteria. The anticipation of a specific transaction by the computer is one of the few known ways of helping determine the correctness of an input item. For example, suppose a receiving report indicates a quantity of 300 units of a product. Even if receiving personnel had no knowledge of how many units were ordered, you can assume the quantity of 300 on the receiving report is accurate if that quantity matches the one on the purchase order.

While there are many systems which tend to create two entries which can be reconciled later, some of them represent such a low level of control that they are almost useless for that purpose. For instance, the withdrawal of inventory is typically supported by the entry on a withdrawal form, which is then posted to a perpetual inventory ledger card. The same amount is posted to some version of an expense ledger. Theoretically, the balances on the ledger cards can be reconciled at any time to the physical balances as represented by an actual count of inventory. But that process can realistically take place only once in a while. Furthermore, it shows only the *amounts* involved and usually tells nothing about who, when, why, and how—information that is necessary to improve control.

Much of the control needed in source data preparation is due to the conversion method used, such as keypunching, which may introduce numerous errors into source data that had been recorded correctly. So we find that we have to introduce a number of verification procedures such as key-verification and batch totals just to make sure the prior step of conversion went all right.

Sometimes, controls are made too tight or too unrealistic because of ignorance of the operating details of the system. In a school system, for example, several students received grades of "00" in various courses. The reason for this turned out to be that computer programmers did not know that a course grade would occasionally be 100. Even though teachers recorded the grade of 100 and keypunch operators punched the three digits into a card, the computer was programmed to accept only two digits; thus the machine ignored the leftmost digit and printed "00" on the grade report. Perhaps it would have been wiser in this case to accept a three-digit number and reject any value greater than 100.

A situation like this can cause trouble over and above that which is obvious to the students affected. A systems analyst who does not look at this too clearly might instead opt for some version of a batch total to check on data conversion. The problem with that option is that a new cost is created for a method that does not happen to address the problem at hand.

Prenumbered forms can help control the input. For instance, they can make it easy to determine quickly how many transactions have occurred and where they are coming from. This in turn helps in determining accountability. Also, it can help in establishing if any of the forms were misplaced or stolen and from which batch. Although this is not always as effective as one might wish, it is better than nothing. Also, the use of prenumbered documents and the possible need to account for them may cause people to be somewhat more careful about filling them out and avoiding gaps in the sequence.

Transmittal logs can also be important in the proper control of data. A log is simply a sheet of paper that accompanies data. It may contain such information as record counts, control totals, dates received, and a time schedule. Its use can also be effective in determining the status and whereabouts of data.

Data conversion equipment providing various controls can be obtained commercially. For example, there are keypunching machines that contain the features needed to apply a self-checking digit. This means that certain errors can be caught at a very early stage, well before they get to the computer. Also, it is possible to obtain machines that automatically count the number of records keyed and take control totals of any fields desired. This can begin a series of controls that can be followed all through the computer processes to make sure that no data are lost or gained.

Source documents that have already been used (that is, the data contained in them have already entered the system) may be stamped or otherwise canceled to make sure they won't be used again. Some applications may have an easy way to reconcile this process, and others may not. Apparently some accounts-payable systems have paid some bills twice and never experienced any problems whatsoever in a later reconciliation of a file of unpaid bills and a control account of the total outstanding. This indicates a poor paying system as well as a poor method of reconciling; when such a situation is detected, it is usually by accident on the part of accounts-payable personnel or by auditors. In any event, there are some systems in which there is no obvious balance that would be disrupted if a transaction were processed twice. In an application that involves a subsequent process such as the taking of a physical inventory, it would be recognized that something was wrong, but it might be hard to pin down exactly what caused it. Thus an "adjusting" entry would be used to reduce the account balance to that evidenced by the physical inventory, but one would never be sure what happened to cause the difference.

Current transactions can be controlled to some extent by comparing them to historical data. While the present amounts may not necessarily have to be related to the past, such comparison can be a worthwhile effort. The more you try to do this on a detail basis, the greater a problem you will have in maintaining enough detail history to make it possible. In some cases, the budgets of current plans would be a more meaningful base than historical actuals.

Sometimes all the controls seem to be in place, but they still fail to work. Consider the case in an Eastern city where a resident got a car excise tax bill for $290,000. It seems that the person keying up the value for the applicable car punched the letter "P" instead of a zero as part of the current value of the car. Because of the manner in which the computer worked, that alphabetic character was converted to a large numerical value, and the individual's car was valued as $7,000,950 instead of $950. Because the total valuation of all cars was too high, the tax rate was calculated at too low an amount on all cars. By the time the error was discovered, it was too late to revise the tax rate upward, and the city was not able to collect some $290,000 of revenue it was planning on.

Of course it is interesting to speculate as to how such an error could get all the way through the system. Officials of the city stated that there were five different places in the system where the error should have been caught. It was in fact caught at one place. But when a corrected punched card was prepared, the new one was torn up and thrown away and the original card with the error was left in with all the other data.

The fact is that although there are some automated methods that will catch errors, it is usually only a manual method that can correct them and reenter data.

Users should have the ultimate responsibility for data control. Certainly, users have a larger stake in data accuracy than does the computer center. To swing into this direction causes some obvious shifts in thinking. Users have to know more about what's happening in the computer center, and the computer center will have to think much more in terms of providing the services required by their users.

The adoption of this concept could spur a movement to develop a *control department* that would not be under the control of the computer center. If this approach is taken, it is suggested that the control department be given plenty of power and that its role be clearly understood by everyone.

This comment on the control department is not restricted to the topic of just raw input data but applies to data files as well.

AUDITING DATA GENERATION AND CONVERSION

As mentioned previously, there are many man-hours of effort and a great range of diverse people involved in the data generation areas. Too often there is practically no audit to speak of in those areas, and frequently most of the attention is given to the conversion stage. This may result in far more money being spent than the results can justify. And often the controls used are not appropriate to the situation as we will see below.

Accuracy

Our first concern here is with the original recording of data. Just what is the most common type of recording error? While one may be led to believe that it is a simple transposition of two adjacent digits (recording, say, 1234 as 1324), a study reported in the May 1963 issue of *Business Automation* (now called *Infosystems*) reported otherwise. In that study, over 8 million transactions were traced in a banking system. Over 60 percent of the recording errors were plain substitutions, such as writing 183 instead of 153. Transpositions accounted for only 1.5 percent of all recording errors.

Armed with the information from that study or from one made currently within the organization, a concerted effort can be made to do the best thing about recording errors. Obviously, some controls work in some situations where other controls may be of no value. Once you know what the enemy is, you can do something constructive about it. In any event, you must be quite cautious as to what and how much you assume about the nature and causes of errors with which you're dealing.

Much of an auditor's test for accuracy in recording functions is going to focus on determining whether the system is set up and operating reasonably well. Of course, an auditor could always compare the data on one set of paperwork to that on another, but agreement there does not directly prove that the data were originally prepared correctly according to the transactions that actually took place. For example, an auditor can

RAW DATA GENERATION AND DATA CONVERSION 147

verify that a store's requisition was neatly filled out, signed, cashed, delivered to accounting, posted to a cost ledger, and finally posted to a perpetual inventory ledger. But all that doesn't prove that particular quantity of that particular item had been issued. In short, the physical aspects of a system and much of the paperwork allegedly reporting on it can be a very troublesome area.

Much of the auditing in that respect could be an observation of how the system appears to work. Included in the audit would be the procedures involved in purchasing, issuing of materials, and the ultimate physical inventories of supply and fixed asset systems. Access to complaints could also be valuable, since they tend to indicate common errors.

As stated earlier, it is often assumed that the initial recording is correct and that the major control and hence auditing issues should begin after that point. This may be acceptable if the transaction authorization part of the system has been checked out and found to be appropriate. In an area such as payroll, for instance, you may partially rely on employees to complain if they are paid too little and on management actions, systems design, and certain control processes to make sure they aren't paid too much.

Checking out the data conversion process is something quite different. Here, the problem is to determine, first, what the system has been designed to verify, and then, if the method chosen catches what it is supposed to. For example, key verification is designed specifically to catch conversion errors. It is an effective method, though at a high cost.

A key question is, is there much of a chance that an operator can fake the key verification process? First, there may not be much of a reason to, unless a verify operator also happens to have been the person who keypunched the data originally. Because of the way the machine is designed, the operator cannot accurately determine what is punched—that person could only guess what is there in an attempt to pass it through the machine. On the other hand, the key-verifier operator can leave cards containing known errors in the deck and pass them on to the next phase of the operation. An important consideration is this: Is there a place in the system where a person absolutely has the job to pull out incorrectly punched cards and see that they are corrected? The key-verifier operator may not have any incentive to do this.

So much of EDP auditing is a test for compliance—is there a reasonable system in effect? Through observation and interviews, the auditor determines whether or not the system is being followed. Presumably, the relevant procedures involve a lot of signatures, initials, and tick marks, and the auditor is checking to see if they have been used as specified. There may also be statistics that show the sources and causes of errors. Perhaps these can be used to help reduce errors in the future.

Many EDP auditing procedures appear to be set up around the use of a checklist. The checklist form is set up as a series of questions. These questions are generally set up so that a yes answer signifies a desirable situation and a no answer suggests the opposite. Any no answer requires some pertinent comments and calls for some special tests to be performed or perhaps carries with it an instruction to go to another section of the form and answer some additional related questions.

At this point I want to concentrate on a question to which the answer is typically yes. It may be quite easy to check that answer and yet overlook something that is significant, such as the quality of the action or its cost-effectiveness. The situation I have in mind relates to key verification. I have seen some auditors who have set out to determine if key verification is used. When told that it is, they mark the appropriate box on the form, make a mental note that data conversion is all right, and then proceed to the next topic. But there are some other questions that should be asked. For example: Is each field of data verified? And are all transactions always verified for that application? If not, what sampling technique is used? This is not meant to suggest that there should always be 100 percent key verification of all data. But it would be good for the auditor to find out how the system is supposed to work.

Even if key verification is found to be adequately performed, however, this does not guarantee that source data are accurate. The auditor should keep in mind that key verification doesn't catch errors in source data but only errors made in keypunching. This statement comes as a surprise to many people. Another issue is what the key-verifier machine actually does. There is one key verifier on the market (fortunately not all) that works as follows: the machine signals a satisfactory situation if the character being checked is present; no attention is paid to any other holes that may be present in that column. To become quite specific, the digit *1* is represented by a single hole in row one of a card column. The alphabetic character *A* is represented by two holes in a single card column, one in row one and another in row twelve. Assume an *A* was mistakenly punched, but the operator is verifying for the digit *1* (an error was made in the original punching of the card; an extra hole somehow got punched). The key verifier would confirm that a *1* is present, but the subsequent computer processing would of course handle the data in that column as an *A*. There are processes that can be used later to detect if an alphabetic character is present where one should not appear. But if those processes aren't used or aren't working, or if in fact an alphabetic character is generally permissible in that position but shouldn't be there in this case, some disastrous processing can result.

Another major issue relates to the ability of key-verifier operators to give the impression that the data were key-verified properly when in fact they were not. The auditor needs to learn what circumvention methods are possible and if in fact any of them are being used.

Whatever else is examined in auditing the data conversion process, the cost-effectiveness aspect should be looked at as well. While a process such as key verification may do an excellent job, it is quite costly. Perhaps the batch total process would work almost as well. A key issue is whether the batch total can be prepared as the by-product of some other necessary operation. It is situations like this that make it necessary for an auditor to know a system well in addition to having a good knowledge of available techniques. Only then can the auditor do more than just mark yes or no; he or she is in a position to recommend improvements.

None of the above discussion about checklists is intended to discourage their use. The intent here is to help auditors make better use of checklists. In fact, I encourage auditors to look at all available checklists in order to pick up various ideas that would not otherwise come to mind.

Should an auditor show a checklist he or she intends to use to those whose work is to be audited? In my opinion, the answer is yes. A major purpose of an audit, in my view, is to improve an operation; if an operating group can clean up various deficiencies before the audit proper begins, so much the better. It is important, however, that any checklist circulated for that purpose will not be considered a long-term contract representing the only issues that will be raised between the parties.

One last point to check in auditing this segment of the system for accuracy is what is done with erroneous data. Supposedly they are sent back to be punched again. Find out if they are, and then also determine if they are reverified. They should be, particularly since it is known that error correction processes themselves have a higher error rate than the original execution.

Auditing of any computer editing processes should be quite straightforward. Get a sample of the editing printout forms, and trace through the system to make sure that all the signaled errors were in fact corrected.

Efficiency

Haven't we all witnessed a situation in a department store where the checkout clerk in lane A is recording credit sales transactions about twice as fast as the clerk in lane B? Is that situation within the province of an EDP auditor? The answer probably depends on the breadth of the mandate provided by management in authorizing the scope of the audit.

I do not intend to resolve the issue here as to whether or not that action should come under the jurisdiction of the EDP auditor. But data generation does represent a significant cost to the organization, and it should be checked by some auditing system, just as every other aspect of operation is. My suspicion is that few EDP auditors look at the recording function with efficiency in mind.

With regard to data conversion activities, there appears to be plenty that can be done with regard to efficiency. With hundreds of thousands of keypunch and related machines having been in use for many years, it has become quite practical to develop some realistic standards. This is realistic even though consideration has to be given to the relative amount of personnel training, legibility of the source documents, and the quality of supervision.

While an audit of the speed of each operator could become quite detailed, such precise measures are rarely required. Instead, an audit of this activity can usually proceed in a broad fashion and still yield data accurate enough to make the necessary decisions.

We have all seen cases, perhaps most often in clerical areas, where the output of two different employees clearly varied by as much as 100 percent or more, yet where the pay scales of the two people did not vary more than a trifle. Here is an area in which some organizations have made substantial gains by instituting some type of incentive program. Unfortunately, incentive programs sometimes end up costing the employer considerably more money without creating a reasonable return. However, the situation described above often is allowed to persist because it is easier to manage that way—it seems easy and "fair" to treat everyone about the same. In fact, this often results in the output of the good workers sliding down to the level of the slower ones.

If you are in business to make money, then you've got to do things differently. You have to find out what it takes to get keypunch operators to work as fast as they can, with continued accuracy, and not just maintain the minimum acceptable pace. A possible incentive would be a pay scale based upon a combination of accuracy and speed. The system could be set up so that employer and employees share in the benefits of the improvement.

There is another issue which is most important in the data conversion process. In many systems, source data are converted into punch cards. Once verified, the data on the punched cards are converted to tape or disc for computer processing.

The use of a punched card typifies the unit record concept. One card typically contains just one record. This is largely because of the physical inability of the card to hold more data. Partially automated punched-card systems of the past, which are quickly becoming obsolete in today's operations, were often called unit record systems. Then came the computer with the existence of media such as tapes and disc, both of which are capable of holding huge quantities of records in one volume.

The point is that one should be careful not to go overboard applying the unit record concept to the punched card. Don't go out of your way to put only one record on a card if it is practical to combine two or more records on one card. In a keypunching operation where a company was able to keypunch two source transactions onto each card, the company saved $45,000 in card costs each year because it was able to cut card usage in half.

How does one stumble on to the fact that there are opportunities such as this one? You might observe keypunching activities, review keypunching instructions, carefully peruse source documents, or examine punched cards that are being thrown away. Whichever method you use, ask yourself why the job is being done this way and if there is a better way. Total familiarity with the what, how, why, when, and where of the operation is indispensable.

On the other hand, you don't want to improve something that should be eliminated or at least replaced by a better method. If it makes more sense to eliminate the keypunching of cards and to convert to tape or disc directly, then merely adopting a better way to punch cards is not good enough. One has to be well grounded in the available alternative approaches.

Fraud

It may at first appear to be a relatively easy thing for a person in a source area to create a transaction whose purpose is to defraud the employer. Therefore, shouldn't a system contain some reasonable checks and balances to make that action difficult? What is required is to spend a reasonable amount of time during system design thinking about how people might try to record false transactions. Generally, the system should be designed so there is a proper separation of duties—that is, no one person should be allowed to have full control over a specific function.

A sound system of authorizations, sign-offs, and doublechecks should make it difficult to prepare a false source document. And proper control of source documents and the subsequent computer programs should make it difficult for a data conversion operator to create a computer record for a nonexistent source document.

But an auditor who is on the lookout for fraud should not be concerned only about the obvious. For example, the well-known Equity Funding fraud involved the creation of phony insurance policies; in the insurance business, a new policy creates an accounting liability. One of the reasons why the auditors did not catch the fraud in its nine years was that they never considered that anyone would deliberately do anything to *create* liabilities; accounting frauds typically involve the *hiding* of liabilities.

Would there ever be a case where a person wanted to defraud his employer but did not have any personal gain in mind? That is possible, for example, where a disgruntled employee just wants to make life difficult for the employer. This could take the form of various actions causing the firm to overexpand, order too much inventory, lose customers, and the like.

Security

Security in raw data generation and data conversion involves issues such as:

154 AUDITING THE DATA PROCESSING FUNCTION

Maintaining strict control over sensitive source documents.
Restricting certain data generation procedures (for instance, salary and bonus data) to a few authorized people.
Restricting certain data conversion procedures to a few authorized people.
Filing the processed source documents in a safe, easily accessible place until they are no longer needed.

These points must be adequately covered by procedures, either written or not. A minimum of auditor time should be sufficient to find out how the system is supposed to work. To test the system, the auditor may rely to some extent on questioning appropriate people. At some point, however, observation is necessary. It doesn't take much effort to check if a file cabinet is locked or not, for example. (It is a good idea to test such items around vacation time, since at that time security may tend to get a little lax.)

Where a certain data conversion process is especially sensitive, such as in payroll, some auditors have suggested taking it out of its regular area and either setting it up in a specially controlled environment or sending it out to a service bureau where the information is of no intrinsic interest to employees.

Effectiveness

Testing for overall effectiveness involves taking a look at the combined features of accuracy, timeliness, and cost. If adequate quantitative standards have been established for each of these beforehand, it should be a simple matter to find out how effective the data generation and conversion process is.

6

Computer Center Operations

It appears that EDP auditing of computer center activities usually takes up more time than auditing of all other related activities combined. Perhaps one reason for this is that the computer center represents an impressive concentration of equipment; also, this is the "end of the line" for automated data processing activities.

It is questionable how appropriate this emphasis is. Especially if a system has not been well designed or if there isn't good control over source data generation, then naturally computer center operations will leave something to be desired; auditing at the tail end can't make up for deficiencies that are prevalent at prior points.

GOALS

In the most general terms, the goal of a computer center is to accurately and completely process authorized data promptly, according to system design, and at a reasonable cost.

In another sense, the general objective would be to get to the place where management has effective control over all computer resources (if it does not already have such, and chances are that it may not). If it already has that control, then it wants to keep it. More specific objectives might include:

Attempt to prevent errors by action instead of just being in the position of correcting errors on a reaction basis.
Develop a reputation for providing what customers want and ultimately need.
Provide a reasonable audit trail so that all activities can be followed up to the extent necessary.

Each organization can expand upon those goals to a considerable extent. Wherever possible they should be quantified so as to facilitate realistic evaluation of actual results.

Considering the money involved and the potential impact on the organization, the goals should be formulated and agreed to jointly by the computer center and top-level management. Furthermore, care must be taken so that performance goals are realistic and adopted with the proper perspective. If the data processing manager's main objective should be a high "up time" on the computer, that can be accomplished by having either backup equipment or a special arrangement with the hardware vendor that service people be located on site all the time. A manager who wants to meet such an objective may just be able to convince his management to pay for such service, which in either case could become quite expensive.

High up time may not be a worthy goal in itself. It should be carefully weighed against the need for, and total cost of, such service. For example, if a computer center operates just one shift a day with only batch-type work, expecting the computer to be available for seven hours and fifty minutes out of the eight hours available seems to be unrealistic. Working a little overtime would be cheaper than most forms of backup.

Suppose instead that the goal is maximum hours of use per day or per month. This can be too easily accomplished by taking on jobs that don't deserve to be computerized, whether they be business applications or things like the bowling scores. A data processing manager once asked me how to increase hours of use. I facetiously suggested to have a computer program available that would add one, subtract one, add one, subtract one. . . . The program could be switched on when there was nothing else to do, and the hours of use would climb to an amount equal to clock time.

In a similar vein, it is easy to cut average hourly costs by just operating more hours, given that much of computer operations costs are of a fixed nature. (Obviously, the additional variable costs needed can hurt the overall expense situation—but then, is someone watching?)

Apparently some keypunch departments operate on the basis of maximizing key strokes per hour on the part of their operators. Data processing management can cause this dubious goal to be reached by such undesirable practices as:

- Designing an input card in such a way that the current date has to be punched into each card. A duplication feature on the keypunch machine can make this process almost totally automatic, so the operator shouldn't be given too much credit for having achieved something. Furthermore, if the cards are going to be converted to tape or disc anyway, the computer should probably be used to put the date in all the records.
- Poor design of source documents. Source forms could be designed in a way that makes it miserable for source departments to record the input data, yet keypunch operators would be able to function at maximum speed. What we really need is an attitude that will look at an entire organization, not just at each unit as a separate entity.
- Instructing keypunch personnel to punch what they see regardless of any obvious errors or omissions in the source data. While these people may not be qualified or allowed to make any corrections, they certainly are qualified to just pull out any obvious errors. That can eliminate several steps otherwise needed to make a correction.

158 AUDITING THE DATA PROCESSING FUNCTION

The relevant point here is that practically no goal is useful standing by itself. The goal of total profit dollars is no good by itself; to be meaningful, it has to be related to something else such as the profit percent on equity, or on total assets, or on some other relevant base. And there is no reason why the goals in a DP department can't be correlated with others, certainly including those of the organization.

STANDARDS

The typical computer center operation is affected by many acts and events, both internal and external. Examples are power and machine failures, operator errors, poor system design, programming errors, and input errors. Despite the many unpredictable and uncontrollable aspects of a computer center, it is necessary to establish some operating standards. A reasonable list would include the following items:

1. Designate a specific person to be in charge of security. Be sure that this person has developed a disaster recovery plan.
2. Maintain segregation of duties within the computer center according to reasonable rules of accountability and internal control.
3. Do not make major equipment changes more often than every three years, since that would make it impossible to realize an acceptable rate of return on such capital investments.
4. Pretest all efforts adequately, and get assurance from the user that the system is worthy of implementation.
5. Use a cost charge-out system that reasonably reflects costs and also motivates both the computer center and its users to act responsibly.
6. Keep statistics on reruns and clearly define what causes them. Then do what is necessary to reduce them to a reasonable percentage.

These six sample standards are but a small choice taken from hundreds of possibilities. Any list that is adopted will naturally reflect the personal feelings of the people involved, because no "standard" list of standards has yet been developed.

Procedures

The general procedure involved in a computer center is to (1) receive source data from user departments, (2) manipulate these source data along with file data, and (3) issue reports to users, both inside and outside the organization.

In order to perform these functions, the computer center must have specialized equipment available, retain various categories of specialized personnel, and have suitable filing space to keep both data and programs. All these functions and resources are in addition to those enumerated in the preceding two chapters, in particular, the substantial resources devoted to computer program preparation and the conversion of source data to computer-readable form.

Each of the procedures mentioned above can be broken down into many more at a detail level. Also, there is a lengthy list of one-time functions, such as file conversion and testing each program before making it operational.

DOCUMENTATION

As stated before, the purpose of documentation is not only to show how you got from one point to another. The computer center is no different from any of the other areas discussed; it has several distinctively different types of documentation used for different purposes.

One form of documentation is that used for training purposes. Newly hired people can use the material, much of which usually is of a self-instructional, proceed-at-your-own-pace nature. Another type informs an employee what to do under a given set of circumstances. For example, whom does the computer operator call at 3 A.M. when the payroll program doesn't work? Since there are so many things to do in a computer center and thus many places where something can go wrong, including real emergencies, the documentation could become rather lengthy. Also, because of the broadness of operations, it is most likely that the documentation available will not cover every situation, even if extreme care has been taken in preparing it. There are obviously situations where employees must go to management to get unusual issues resolved.

On the other hand, you need to consider the long-range effect on people if there is an answer for every situation in a manual. Causing employees to use such a crutch all the time may hinder their development by denying them the opportunity to reason things out and make some decisions on their own. However, it is unlikely that the manual would be that complete, that employees could always find the relevant passage, or that they would always look there even when they needed to.

You might want to restrict operator access to certain forms of system and program documentation. In this way, it would become quite difficult for the operator to change program steps to the detriment of the organization. Since many computer operators move on to programming positions, it is difficult to prevent them from learning how to write programs, although some organizations have tried to prevent operators from gaining that knowledge. Furthermore, the firm itself may be providing programming instruction to such a person with a promotion in mind. Thus the important thing is to keep current program documentation away from a person who does not have a real need for it.

A second major category of documentation necessary in a computer center is that dealing with the statistics of operating situations. Valuable information would relate to the running times of various jobs, instances of computer down time, detailed operating failures of individual equipment components, the need for and the causes of reruns, and details regarding the level of service provided to users.

COMPUTER CENTER OPERATIONS   161

A third category may relate to details of personnel. This might include such things as individual histories of training, training plans, and periodic evaluations of performance. Also, a plan for a career path would be valuable both to each individual and to the organization as a whole.

COMPUTER CENTER CONTROLS

Controls Built into the Hardware

Some of the most important controls affecting computer center operations are those built into the hardware by the manufacturer. This is the one area that user organizations can generally do the least about.

Newer computer models have generally been designed to operate virtually free of their own errors. Not only are they built so as to commit few errors, but they are also capable of catching any errors they make and even correcting such errors themselves or stopping and displaying an ERROR message on the appropriate unit of the machine. What this means is that you can be relatively, though perhaps not 100 percent, sure that the computer itself will not introduce any errors but do only what it is told to.

There have been a few attempts by those without much computer knowledge to force the manufacturers to provide enough built-in controls to prevent fraud by users. While that may sound nice, such features would probably hinder users from doing all the normal things that have to be done. Fortunately, this thinking has not gotten very far, at least as far as it concerns the possibility of holding computer manufacturers responsible for computer fraud. Appropriate courts have, to date, been quick to dispel such lawsuits, as they should.

In another vein on this point, Robert Patrick, a computer consultant, has performed research and reported that manufacturers have eased up a bit in providing built-in features in the interest of reducing design and manufacturing costs.* His work

* *Computerworld,* June 6, 1977.

has resulted in a National Bureau of Standards report entitled *Performance Assurance and Data Integrity Practices* (NBS Special Publication 500-24). It is obvious that all organizations using computers will have to keep up to date on this issue to make sure they institute their own compensating procedures if the manufacturers should pull back to an undesirable level. This point might in fact become significant enough to affect hardware acquisition decisions.

Input/Output Controls

The first active control consideration is to set up an *input/output control group*. No matter how large a computer center is, it needs this function. In the smallest computer center, the service could be provided by a small fraction of one individual's time; in a large operation, it could involve as many as a dozen people.

It doesn't matter so much whether this group is located inside or right outside the physical location called the computer center as long as it is in the immediate vicinity. The group might report to the director of the computer center or to some other official; but more important than its reporting relationship is that the group exists, has competent people, and does the right things.

Regarding input activities, the control group would do such things as physically receive, log, and perhaps count source data; broadly review input for format and reasonableness; and schedule source data for conversion to computer-readable form. All input should come to this group; nothing should go directly to keypunching or to computer operators. Any output from the computer—whether an edit run requiring correction of errors or completed output ready for distribution—should come to this group for the required distribution. By following these simple rules, the control group will always know where everything is and be in a position to immediately check on its completion status.

Security Controls and Backup

As far as the computer itself goes, there must be controls over temperature, humidity, and power failure. Also, fire, flood, and wind damage are to be considered. The controls required include not only methods to prevent trouble but also recovery methods if trouble should develop. This generally means some kind of formal, tested backup hardware arrangement at another site.

Apparently, many computerized organizations have never really considered the operational consequences if the computer were knocked out of operation for an extended period of time (more than a day or two). (Perhaps some of them have such effective manual backup that it is not an issue.) A useful mental exercise in this regard is to hypothesize that a certain disaster occurs within the next minute. What could or would you do to sustain operations? When you start thinking of all the problems, some of which seem to have no solutions, you begin to see the importance of preventing such trouble within limits of reason.

A major criterion for measuring the value of a control is looking at its cost. Suppose you discover a situation that represents a serious exposure. How are you going to take care of it? One alternative is to do nothing and then, if it should happen, bear the cost of correction or recovery at that time. The other alternative is to remove or reduce the risk, which in itself is going to cost some money. Generally, risk analysis should be used to determine which of the two approaches is preferable.

A company in California applied the risk analysis concept to its insurance policy that covered possible earthquake damage. The policy cost $54,000 annually, and it included a $1 million deductible provision for the life of the policy. The risk analysis yielded these figures:

Chance of loss	Amount of loss
90%	$ 10,000
40%	50,000
4%	800,000

The amount of loss was estimated as an annual amount over the 25-year life of the building. In view of this analysis, the company decided to cancel the insurance and assume all the risk itself.

In disaster recovery, it must be recognized that it may be difficult or impossible to recover current detail data. Assume, for example, that last Friday night all important master, current-balance, and year-to-date files were copied and sent to an off-premises storage site. Since that time, transactions have been coming in from everywhere, mostly in the form of source documents. Keypunching of some transactions has been completed, but it has not yet started on some others. A fire destroys the computer center—and with it all data for the current week—this Thursday afternoon. Would there have been a reasonable way to provide backup for those current data?

If you decide to have such backup, it appears you would have to send out duplicates of data every day (or at even closer intervals), possibly in combination with requiring all source departments to keep copies of all source data, or perhaps microfilm all data before sending them to keypunching. Of course, the data could be destroyed by a fire while in transit from the source to the computer center or while at the site used for microfilming. Here, too, is a good place to apply risk analysis. In any event, the consequences of losing current detail are usually not as severe as those of losing master, balance, or year-to-date files.

The need for backup computer facilities is always a consideration when dealing with computer security. However, the problems involved can be horrendous. In 1977, a group of EDP auditors and interested computer center managers decided to form a "backup association" so as to deal with the issue in an organized and concentrated way. Various organizations put money into a pool that was used to make a study of the problems and at the same time locate a backup facility that would be able to handle each firm's computer work.

One of the first proposals, namely, to establish a new computer center dedicated to this function, was soon abandoned because of the cost. The group ended up selecting a service bureau operation site. It appears that by now a comfortable arrangement has been worked out whereby all details have been taken care of. An interesting feature of the deal is that time has been provided for members of the backup association to test their disaster plans to make sure they can really use the backup equipment.

Security Controls and Employees

Computer security discussions often come around to the story of a person walking through a computer center with a 25-cent magnet in his pocket and erasing all the tapes. Although various versions of this story have been reported, they appear to be inaccurate. Extensive studies by the National Bureau of Standards in 1977 concluded that it would require a large magnet at very close range to cause such damage. ("Very close" here means a couple of inches, with no protective containers being used.)

Although in some respects it may seem desirable to get everyone involved in and concerned about the issue of security, this creates its own dangers; in particular, it will make everybody aware of all the weak spots. In many cases, it would thus be better to involve people only on the basis of their need to know.

There are a number of controls appropriate to employees in general. Many of these controls are direct descendants of historical practices that represent sound internal controls.

One recommended security control is to require everyone to take a vacation every year. One manager told me he requires that to be a minimum of two weeks at a time. His reasoning is that if an employee has been performing in an unauthorized manner, he is likely to get away with it if he is gone only one week, since his work may just be put aside and allowed to wait until he gets back. By contrast, if he is going to be away for two weeks, there is a greater tendency to assign someone else to take over his work. If there is an irregularity, then there is a greater chance it will be caught.

Job rotation is another method that should be considered.

For example, consider switching a computer operator responsible for payroll to production and inventory control. Also, it is generally advisable to switch people around among the various shifts. This is best done on a somewhat irregular basis or at least without giving too much advance notice.

This practice of rotating has the additional advantage of developing people who can handle more jobs, provide backup in all areas, and thus become more valuable to the organization. Also, it reduces the risk of boredom due to sticking to one job too long. On the other hand, it has the disadvantage that you don't gain the economies often possible through specialization of labor. Finally, the possible ill effects of introducing forced changes in assignments or working hours must be considered.

Another essential security control relates to civil disruption or disgruntled employees. A good method to reduce this risk is to stop making the computer center a showcase, considerably reduce or completely eliminate tours, and make it off-limits to all employees except operators and occasionally systems analysts and programmers.

Knowing that the best personnel practices will occasionally fail and a bad person will turn up and operate a system to his own advantage or with the intention to harm his employer, the wise organization will probably obtain bond insurance to recover from employees' acts. In applying for the bonding coverage, there should be some practices learned from or perhaps required by the bonding company that if put into effect will help to control operations.

Efficiency Controls

Efficiency is a relative concept; it refers to how much of a resource was used compared to how much should have been used to achieve a specified result. In a computer center, common bases for calculating efficiency are the time and the related dollars required to run a job. Either base can be relevant both to data processing management and to users.

The strongest control over efficiency is to prepare sound cost estimates. Analysis of the difference between budgeted and actual amounts should bring to light the causes of the discrepancy so that the problem can be corrected and results improved the next time. Analysis of the differences may occasionally suggest that the estimates were too optimistic.

A practice that is getting much more attention is that of charging users some cost for the services they obtain from the computer center. While there are several things to be gained from such a practice, if it is done in one of many incorrect fashions, there can be considerably more harm than good. A major factor determining whether or not it will work is the quality of the organization's financial planning and control system.

Let me illustrate the problem by describing two unsatisfactory systems. In one company, the data processing manager handled the cost allocation largely by himself. He established a standard billing rate per hour and charged out at that rate all year. When he had available his actual costs for the whole year, he found that he had charged users $50,000 too much ("overabsorbed" in accounting terms). When I asked him what happened to the $50,000, he said he just credited it all to the department of his best friend in the company. When I asked him why, he said, "It didn't matter anyway; no one was going to look at it, so why not?" In that company, managers were on a bonus system carefully tied to meeting budgets.

Another company tried to avoid such overcharging by charging out actual costs each month. This not only resulted in the charges not being available until the third week of the following month but also caused this interesting situation. The results were as follows:

Month	Total hours of use	Total costs	Hourly rate	Hours used by Smith	Charges to Smith
August	200	$8,400	$42	45	$1,890
September	182	$8,190	$45	43	$1,935

Smith had an obvious gripe. He used the computer two hours less in September than in August, but was charged $45 more. While there are all sorts of accounting arguments, such as variable vs. fixed costs and idle capacity, that might be used to justify such cost allocations, users quickly get turned off by a situation of that kind. There should not have to be a justification, because it shouldn't have happened.

The starting point should be to establish the purpose to be served by a charging system. If it is just to satisfy an organization policy that all service departments "zero out" their budgets, then that can surely be done in a manner that won't take much effort and won't hurt anyone. Perhaps just follow the procedure that has been used in the past in many other service departments.

A more appropriate reason to charge is to give both users and the computer center an incentive to operate more efficiently, that is, to spend less money or to spend money more effectively. This does not simply mean to lower hourly rates charged by the computer center.

A common reason given for charging costs is to make users aware of the actual cost to the organization of various services. Presumably, this will motivate users to cut out all jobs whose results aren't worth more than the costs of providing them. In such instances, it is necessary to know quite a bit about cost control generally throughout the organization. If it is a simple matter for a user to obtain a larger budget just because of increased costs from the computer center, then this may not directly cause a reduction in requested efforts. For this to work well, then, users must have some way to quantify the value of jobs so they can be compared to the costs of providing them. This is obviously difficult on jobs such as payroll and accounts payable which presumably have to be performed without the opportunity to perform a true cost-benefit analysis.

The use of the *checkpoint* as a means of aiding efficiency was described in Chapter 1.

File Conversion

File conversion typically involves taking a file of data in paper form, such as ledger cards, and transferring it to a form the computer can handle, such as punched cards, tape, or disc.

It could also refer to a conversion among cards, tape, or disc—that is, transferring data from one of those forms to another form. A third possibility is to convert within a certain medium, such as from one tape to another tape that has a different recording density per inch or uses a different electronic structure to represent data. The major problems are associated with the type mentioned first, since so much manual effort is required.

The major problems involved in file conversion relate to timeliness and accuracy. Typically you are using one system one day and want to use the new system the next day, either for parallel testing purposes or for a complete switch.

The first thing to do is to establish a detailed schedule determining who is to do what steps in what sequence and by what date. Make sure the people and the equipment are all set to go. Computer programs are also almost always involved. For example, the computer may be reading the source data from punched cards and writing those data out to magnetic tape. While doing so, the computer should be counting the number of transactions and taking totals on relevant fields. All this means that special programs must be obtained and tested.

All the pieces of the conversion must be tested as a unit to make sure it works. Keypunch personnel must become familiar with the source data, and computer programs must be precisely written to handle the data formats. The proper equipment and supplies must be available. The key is to "walk it through" on paper first and then test it thoroughly.

One data processing manager thought he had provided for everything needed to make a clean conversion. This conversion plan relied on using the computer facilities of a neighboring company. Imagine his surprise when he got there and found the computer configuration did not include an automatic card punch, which was essential for his operations! In the hustle of activity, he and his staff had completely overlooked the need for that piece of equipment. Since they had never simulated the conversion, it was not obvious what was lacking. It took another two weeks to locate the proper equipment and to make new arrangements.

With regard to accuracy, we want to make sure that no account is lost in the conversion and that both the amounts and the identification code(s) of each account are handled correctly.

How can you make sure each account is converted correctly? One thing to do is to take a record count. Count the number of records before the conversion; have the computer count how many records there are after conversion. If any records are lost or gained, that should be immediately apparent. Another control is the batch total. Get a total of each relevant field of the data before conversion. Then have the computer provide a similar total of each relevant field from the computerized data. Compare totals and reconcile any differences.

It would have to be an unusual situation where there is no convenient way to obtain a record count and a batch total amount. However, be careful to avoid the mistake made by a major company several years ago, which took a total on accounts receivable from ledger cards, punched computer cards from the ledger cards, and then got a total accounts receivable from the computer cards. The people responsible for the conversion immediately recognized they were some $4 million short on the amount side, but by that time the old ledger card file had already been destroyed and there was no backup available. Clearly, a situation like that is hard to explain to stockholders.

Making sure the identification codes are converted correctly might be handled by key verification, for example. However, this method doesn't tell if any records happen to be missing. A more suitable technique is the *hash total:* Add the account numbers of the old records, then have the computer get a total of the account numbers of the converted data. (Note that the name hash total is appropriate because the total of the account numbers is not otherwise a meaningful number.) This technique will catch not only transcription mistakes, but also a situation where a record was misplaced. If necessary, it can be made more practical by splitting a large file into smaller workable batches.

When making a conversion, it is also important to make sure

you are working with correct and reasonably current data. For example, it is undesirable to convert accounts receivable that have no hope of collection or inventory balances for which a physical count hasn't been taken for several years. In the accounts-receivable application, have a responsible financial person go through the accounts and reject accounts, for example, that have been outstanding more than a year. In the inventory control area, management should insist that a current physical inventory be taken to assure that sound data are used.

In a manual accounts-payable system, the total of the unpaid bills in the "TO PAY" drawer did not equal the figure appearing in the general ledger control account. This condition was known only to the manager of accounts payable. When the conversion to computer form took place, the discrepancy became known to the computer center manager. Unfortunately, he did nothing to correct the situation but instead covered up the error. The internal auditor subsequently found the error and reported both offenders to the controller, who instituted a stricter system of sign-offs in all cases where one person was passing data to another person or department. That step resulted in people acting in a more responsible manner and covering up less for the mistakes of others.

File Protection

While there are many things that can cause the loss of a data file, including fire, flood, and theft, the largest risk is the errors made by computer personnel as they perform their daily functions. Fire, flood, and theft involve loss in a physical sense, whereas errors by personnel most often involve erasure of the data—the tape itself is still available, but without the required data.

The data on any reel of magnetic tape or any disc file usually become "worthless" after a period of time as new data come along to supersede the previous. For example, both year-to-date totals and master files are rendered out of date merely due to the passing of time and the creation of new transactions. Since a medium such as magnetic tape can be used over again for new data by simply erasing what was there before, you

Figure 11. A reel of tape and its file protect ring.

must make sure the erase and write-over are done at the right time. If done prematurely, then data you want to retain may have been destroyed. Although there may—indeed should—be a backup file, you don't want to have to go to backup when prevention of trouble would have been a smarter way to go.

A physical device developed to help reduce the risk of premature file erasure is the *file protect ring* shown in Figure 11. Observe that the file protect ring has a small tip. When the ring is placed in a groove in the back of the tape reel and the tape reel then placed in a tape drive, the tip on the ring pushes against a switch on the tape drive. It is only when that switch is pushed that the tape drive can operate in a mode that allows writing new data on that reel of tape.

To prevent accidental erasure, then, operators are instructed to use the ring only when old data are to be erased and replaced with new data. This is an example of a positive control; the operator has to *do* something specific to cause erasure.

How safe is the use of the file protect ring? On a scale of zero to 100, how many points do you give it? The typical answer I get is in the area of 10 points; a few people go as high as 90 to 95. Its effect is only as good as the employee involved. If the employee should lack reasonable intelligence, be tired, lack motivation, or have insufficient training, use of the file protect ring is likely to be unsatisfactory.

A technique that usually does a much better job is the use of internal labels. An internal label is a word or code magnetically written at the front of a file when the file is created. Every time the file is used by the computer, steps in the program check the word or code at the front of the tape to make sure that the tape is being used only when it should be; otherwise, the computer stops and reports the error to the operator. Thus you take much of the control away from the computer operator and give it to the programmer. If both internal labels and the file protect ring are used, premature file destruction should be eliminated.

Auditors will generally favor the use of the label approach. Not only is the level of protection much greater, but it is easier for the auditor to determine that the feature is used in all applicable programs, where it will work all the time. If an auditor were to observe how effectively the computer operator used the file protect ring, the auditor might be satisfied with his observations but still wonder about the level of protection at those times the operator was not being observed.

It is an interesting question as to what an auditor should do when it is discovered that a computer center doesn't use labels at all. Instead of making an immediate push to get them to initiate the use of labels, the auditor should probably first study the situation carefully. Find out why labels haven't been used and the amount of work needed to put them into use.

AUDITING COMPUTER CENTER OPERATIONS

In any audit of a computer center, a major effort should be made to review the documentation that is kept about operations within the department. Of particular importance are such things as equipment failure, the need for reruns, and the causes of errors. Each of these items needs to be examined to see if management took some reasonable action to either eliminate or reduce the cause. If there is no such documentation, then the auditor should recommend that it be started.

Another item to be carefully reviewed is the console log provided by the computer as an offshoot of normal processing. This log is a list that is printed by the operating system to serve as the major communication between operator and computer. The computer typically requests certain information for each job to be run; it would be valuable to double-check those requests and see what the operator's responses were. Additionally, the computer reports on certain errors, and it is desirable to see how many there were and what, if anything, the operator did about them.

As an example, if the job instructions in the documentation say that a critical aspect of operation, such as a printout to the operator with a certain request, is to be handled a certain way, the auditor will want to check if actual practice conforms to that rule.

Accuracy

There are many things an auditor can do to test for the accuracy within computer center operations. If the auditor is at all close to a situation, there will be enough rumors and comments floating about concerning the accuracy of the EDP system. If that doesn't provide any information, interviewing selected users almost certainly will. At some point, however, those comments will have to be properly evaluated to separate fact from fiction.

Another useful technique is to test the computer runs that are in fact reruns, since many of those are due to the job having been run incorrectly the first time. By identifying the more common causes of reruns, the auditor can hopefully reduce the need for such reruns in the future.

To get a better handle on the accuracy problem, the auditor

may also review the incoming mail in the user departments to track down the incidence of complaints and the requests for adjustments among customers and vendors as well as internal departments. The most effective way to do this would be for the auditor to have all incoming mail routed to him, just as a financial auditor may request the organization's bank to mail the checking account statement and canceled checks directly to the auditor.

A data processing operation involves the flow of data from one point to another. As discussed previously, the system should be designed to include distinct checkpoints that monitor and control that flow of data. If it is, then the auditor can test those checkpoints as they relate to the flow of data. Typical controls would be record counts and batch totals. These should be set up in such a way that they can be verified even where other units of data merge in or where units of data leave the main stream of flow.

There are two tests that are a central part of the typical financial audit: (1) do the books balance? and (2) what types of adjusting entries are a normal part of the processing routine? Those tests can be used by the EDP auditor as well. It should be noted, though, that testing if the books balance is not so much a question of balancing credits against debits; the more important issue is whether detail records in subsidiary ledgers balance to control records.

As a final point, it is not enough just to determine that the system performs accurately; the time and effort spent in obtaining that accuracy must be considered as well. In other words, the auditor must be concerned with the cost-effectiveness of accuracy. Pinpointing the reasons for any excessive costs should help an auditor to suggest steps that would enable users to obtain the required accuracy on the first pass, not as a result of a great deal of rework.

Efficiency

Recent computer literature has stressed the point that hardware costs have been declining. That is certainly true when you compare hardware costs to the costs of labor; hardware costs as a percentage of total costs have been dropping for many years. Because of increased computer speeds and breakthroughs in manufacturing technology, the cost of an individual instruction has likewise fallen. However, few computer centers have seen a total cost decline. One reason is that high-level programming languages of today operate less efficiently than the languages of a few years ago. Hence, it often takes more machine time now to run a comparable job. Also, today's typical computer center handles more work than its predecessors, so although the cost per calculation may be down, there are more calculations. Personnel costs are rising so fast at the same time there are declines in hardware costs that total costs are probably up. If a cost reduction was forecast and the actual system is not producing it, this is usually a result of poor reasoning in original design and not necessarily of poor execution.

Another item to be wary of is any claims by others regarding their cost levels. For instance, suppose the controller of Company A meets the controller of Company B, who says it costs an average of 42 cents to issue a payroll check in his company. That may not be a target at all for Company A to try to reach. Perhaps there are so many differences between the organizations, including their internal costing procedures, that it is useless to make any such comparisons. The point here is that an auditor has to be careful how information relative to one situation will be allowed to influence him or her in another situation.

As a final item to be cautious about, don't spend much time comparing this year's costs to last year's in an effort to study efficiency. The computer industry, in addition to industry in general, has been just too dynamic in recent years to allow simple comparisons of that kind. Furthermore, comparing actual costs tends to establish the previous year as a standard, which may not be reasonable at all.

Now that we have seen what not to do, let's look at the positive side. The most powerful thing to do is to compare an actual operation to the budget that has been set up for that period. (Of course, this assumes that operating people had something to say about the budget that was adopted for them.) My personal feeling is that most people have so much pride in themselves and their work that they will not request money at a high rate just so they can take it easy later and spend all the money. If anything, computer specialists have been so optimistic, they have developed budgets on the low side.

Comparison of actual data to budget data must carefully take into account the causes and the available alternatives.

One must realize that the use of considerable overtime is not inherently bad. The automotive industry has used it effectively where the alternative would be to hire more full-time people, who would eventually have to be laid off when business declined. For the auditor, the important thing is to determine the cause of overtime, whether that be excessive reruns, down time, poor scheduling, or perhaps inefficiency due to poor training or employment of incompetent people.

The problem of computer reruns has been mentioned repeatedly. This area may need to be examined in depth. The seriousness of the problem is often hushed up, but some people admit that reruns are necessary for as many as 30 percent of all computer runs.

It seems to me that some people go out of their way to cover up certain problems, and this is certainly one of them. In any event, operating logs should clearly identify what run was a rerun and the reason for performing the rerun. Someone should collect data as to the causes, even if that person has to be the auditor. Here again, the purpose of collecting such information is not to punish but to improve results.

Common causes of reruns include user requests, errors in data conversion, late data, computer operator errors, software errors, and hardware malfunctions. Once the statistics are developed, then solutions can be proposed. However, some amount of reruns is normal, and the costs of preventing reruns altogether would be significant.

In an audit at a manufacturing company, the internal auditor found that computer operator errors were the main cause for reruns. One suggestion he made was that operators should be "charged" the standard internal hourly rate for each such rerun. An applicable change was made in the system. Under the new system, an operator was to be dismissed when the total of charges reached a specified limit in a given time period. That charging method was given credit for making a substantial improvement in both efficiency and effectiveness.

Quite often the issue of efficiency depends on very technical details of what is happening in the machine at any time. Some firms approach this problem by getting a hardware monitor. This is a device that can determine when and how much of the time certain electronic components are busy or waiting for some other action to occur. Conceivably, the hardware monitor would indicate that under the circumstances, certain components should be replaced by either faster or slower components. The proper use of a hardware monitor is beyond the scope of the typical EDP auditor but instead within the province of a highly qualified technician.

A data processing manager may have decided to obtain a hardware monitor for use in managing a computer center. If the proposal to obtain a hardware monitor should come from an auditor, then help could be obtained from a consultant who specializes in that field.

Security

The auditor's role is not restricted to checking that a system is operating according to the way it was designed. Quite often the design is defective, and that should be identified along with a suggestion for improvement.

For example, in most computer centers today, it should be obvious that no one other than operators should be allowed in the computer center. If there is presently no rule against access by other people, then it is up to the auditor to propose such a rule. On the other hand, if there is such a rule, then the auditor will want to see if it is enforced. This may be checked by interviewing people, reviewing documentation, and possibly by observation. On the many occasions when the auditor is in the computer center in the normal course of conducting the audit, there will be many attempts by others to enter; it is a simple matter to observe how these cases are handled.

Another tactic is for the auditor to get a person to try to enter. A CPA firm routinely instructed their newly hired auditors to try to enter computer centers of the firm's clients. The new auditor would typically pose as a new salesperson for the computer manufacturer. Several of the clients learned very emphatically (but cheaply) how dangerous it is to admit anyone dressed in a suit and carrying an attaché case into the computer center and give him full license to roam about.

The surprise visit, particularly to the second and third shift, should also occasionally be used. Although this technique may be repulsive to some people who feel they should always be fully trusted, it's useful to remember that people with physical control over cash have always lived with this threat and have been perfectly able to survive. Computer center personnel should be able to accept it as a way of life as well.

Again, a computer center should have some sort of disaster plan that would permit a continuation or restart of operations if trouble should occur. If there is no such plan, then one should be proposed by the auditor.

If there is a plan, it should be reviewed to see how well it is designed. In this context, a management consulting firm claims in an advertisement that 95 percent of the disaster plans in existence don't work. Perhaps this is an area for some fruitful research.

No matter how well-designed the disaster plan appears, the only real test is to see how it works in an emergency. This calls for a simulation of a disaster. Walk into the computer center unannounced and say that X percent of the room has just been destroyed by a fire (bomb, flood). What is everybody supposed to do to get operating again within a certain number of hours? It won't take long to determine how well set up the center is to effectively recover. When one firm tried this, it was discovered that some employees couldn't lift the fire extinguishers from the hooks on the wall.

The typical disaster plan is likely to overlook some important features. For example, access to supplies such as pre-printed computer forms and accounts-payable checks may not have been considered. In the testing area, there has historically been enough confusion to suggest that employees have not received adequate training.

Fraud

The publicized cases of computer fraud show a poor record of detection by an auditor. (Hopefully auditors have found some instances of fraud that just didn't get publicized.) It seems that fraud typically is detected by accident or perhaps because of excessive greed on the part of the thief. In view of the fact that the detection rate has not improved considerably in recent years, it would seem that there are not many specific instructions one could give to an auditor to solve that problem. Nonetheless, I believe there are a few suggestions that should be of help.

I believe that a starting point is to carefully review the functioning of the input/output control group. Determine if all input and output are controlled to the point where a computer operator would have a difficult time inserting input or withdrawing output unnoticed by anybody. Assume that the input/output control group has a count of the source data. Also assume that program steps get a count of the data processed by the computer. Then by all means reconcile the two counts to make sure no data have been added between those points. There have been many cases of computerized systems that begin control at the point where the data first enter the computer, not before that, where it should begin.

Once a fraudulent transaction is entered, the crook may not need to do anything more to reap the benefits. Thus, in the fraudulent system depicted in Figure 2, John Doe just sits back and waits for the fraudulent check to be delivered to him in the regular check distribution procedure.

The important point is that any slight difference in anything should be completely investigated to make sure what caused it. For example, a payroll fraud involved taking a penny from everyone else and transferring the full amount to the crook's account. When an employee asked about the penny difference on his pay, he was told by management (without any investigation on its part) that it was a computer rounding error and "you know the trouble we've had with the computer."

In the Equity Funding fraud, auditors asked for specific information that one would expect an organization to have readily at hand. However, management had intentionally suppressed the retention of paper files, so the auditors were often told that the data would be available the following day. Then Equity Funding management would hold an all-night "fraud party" to develop the data that would satisfy the auditors. Perhaps the auditors should have been more aggressive in seeing source data and reports now rather than always having to wait until the next day.

It appears that the most popular of the computer frauds is the theft of services, specifically, performing computer work for outsiders to the financial benefit of the crook. In a classical case, the entire third shift was used for that purpose. The defrauded company paid for the space, the computer, the computer operator, and most of the supplies. About the only item supplied by the crook was the billhead he used to charge his customers.

Even if management can be deceived into thinking the organization should have three shifts of computer operation when there is only enough work for two shifts, an auditor should be able to detect a problem in this area. Surely there are, or at least should be, enough work schedules, batches of input and output, and computer logs to indicate discrepancies of this dimension. Also, surprise visits at unusual hours, both by management and auditor, should uncover—or, even better, prevent—such frauds.

Another fraud that has attracted some attention is the sale of duplicate copies of valuable files. An example of such a file would be a mailing list of prospective customers. Since it may be difficult to search employees to make sure they aren't leaving with a whole or partial copy of a file (would it be easy for a crook to mail it out of the building?), perhaps the best thing to do is to make it difficult to get such a copy made.

Although it is a normal procedure to make copies of files (for example, for backup purposes), the procedure can be monitored as to what files may be copied by whom and when. One might even have a bell ring or lights flash when a particular master file is being copied. Reviewing the computer log for the use of a copying program should pinpoint when there was a potential offense, which can then be tracked down. Just the knowledge that there are some controls and follow-up procedures and that there will be strong disciplinary action helps prevent fraudulent acts at least to some extent.

Most of the above comments apply to a fraud situation where just one person is involved. If several people decide to work together to the detriment of the organization, that is much more difficult to defend against. One helpful technique is to determine if all books and accounts balance. If they don't an investigation is warranted to discover the reason.

If the books do balance, then perhaps there are some accounts that are out of line. Accounting entries may have been made (or, more likely, have been included in regular entries) that cause all values to balance out. Investigations of unusual balances and comparisons of actual to budgeted amounts are methods of learning about unusual activities.

Overall Effectiveness

In determining how well overall computer operations are working, answers should be obtained from users to the following questions:

What is the general user attitude?
Do users request new systems? (If so, that may indicate a certain amount of trust in internal operations.)

COMPUTER CENTER OPERATIONS 183

Do users tend to seek help from outside the organization? (If they do, that suggests a poor operation.)

Do users usually have their own backup systems? Do they tend to hang on to their manual system even after it has been computerized?

Are there frequent requests for changes in current systems and is there a pattern in these requests? Are they concentrated in specific applications, where individuals can be identified as being at fault?

Another major question concerns the nature of the applications that have been computerized. Has the organization simply computerized the traditional clerical applications, or has it installed systems for the basic functions that represent the backbone of the organization? For most organizations, the real payoffs are not in payroll and accounts payable but in those functions that maintain the customer base, inventory control, and production scheduling.

Finally, another matter of particular interest within the computer center might be to review the career path plans for the various employees and to check turnover statistics to see if the organization is reasonably holding on to qualified people. Proper attention to employee development will help avoid the heavy hiring and training costs associated with high turnover.

The Integrated Test Facility (ITF)

An auditor naturally wants to test a system to see how it works, from creating specific source documents to the issuing of reports. The question is how to go about it in a realistic way. Will some dummy transactions be created and processed in a separate run of applicable programs? If so, that is not like the real thing. On the other hand, processing test data in a regular run together with real data is not practical, because it would upset regular processing and related totals as well as real files.

An auditing technique that has been developed to solve this problem is the *integrated test facility* (ITF), also known as the *minicompany approach*. A set of account numbers is designed, just as if the firm were setting up operations for a new subsidiary. Fictitious transactions are created for that set of accounts. Regular processing takes place, including updating of files and printing of reports. But since all the transactions relate to that specific minicompany, those dummy accounts are not used at all when the firm consolidates the data into financial reports. Thus all the processing steps within the company can be thoroughly tested, but the sample transactions will not contaminate the real data.

7

Other Issues

This chapter discusses a number of additional but not necessarily related topics. The first of these in particular, maintenance of systems and programs, may for some organizations be as important as any of those in the previous chapters.

SYSTEM AND PROGRAM MAINTENANCE

Once systems and their related procedures and computer programs are installed and working, there will be requests for myriad changes to be made. In some cases it will be recognized that errors were made in certain of the processes that led to installation, or certain conditions—particularly laws and regulations—may have changed and require appropriate modifications of EDP programs, systems, or procedures. Also, users may want something different, or operating specialists may see an opportunity for improvement. All these items add up to so much that in computer programming alone, many organizations report that 50 percent or more of all programming efforts is spent on maintenance.

Goals

The goals of system and program maintenance are to review all major aspects of all systems, propose changes where appropriate, and promptly make those changes that have been authorized. Also, there should be a constant review of all standing policies to make sure that they aren't causing more harm than good.

It's essential to make sure that all changes are made only with proper approval, because of all the havoc caused when unauthorized changes are made—and I am referring not only to changes that represent fraudulent actions but to the common everyday problems that arise somewhere else even though conditions may be all right in the immediate area of the change. While these changes may be made with perfectly honest and good intentions, many people don't understand the potential impact of a local change on the total organization. That's why changes must be approved by a designated individual or group of people with the required expertise and broader outlook.

Standards

There are certain standards that, if adhered to, will help assure that system and program changes are effective. Examples are:

- All requests for changes should be in writing, and any resulting implementation should be subject to the same controls as the original design.
- All requests for changes should be carefully reviewed by a *change committee* composed of from three to five responsible persons. Only changes authorized by the change committee should be instituted.
- Changes other than those required to comply with new laws or regulations should be approved only if there is some promise that they will be cost-effective. The cost-benefit analysis should consider the cost to put the change into effect, the expected value of doing so, and the length

of time the change could be in effect, given the expected life cycle of the application.
- All new systems and all changes to existing systems should be subject to a postimplementation audit within six months after installation. Staffing of the audit department will be such as to meet the requirement of this standard.

Procedures and Controls

The requests for changes in most aspects of an operation typically begin within minutes after any decision has been made and continue until the end of the system's life cycle. Although these requests, both formal and informal, for changes may come from everywhere, the majority will probably be made by the users of the output of the system. There will probably be a scarcity of requests from such people as keypunch and computer operators. There may be a tendency on the part of some programmers to go back and redo a programming routine because they just figured out a way to reduce the total program by a few instructions and thus save a few microseconds for each record to be processed.

Whereas programming changes of the type last mentioned are hardly justified, there are some system changes that can be quite worthwhile. One would be to eliminate any unnecessary steps of source data preparation. Once it has been determined that a particular manual procedure has no value, it makes sense to cut it off. This can usually be done without much trouble—certainly more easily than changing or adding programs, for example. In general, a change such as making a source document easier to use or a report more readable can have good payoffs.

In many cases, the real reason for the deluge of change requests is that the original design was not done in the proper manner and did not include all the necessary features realistically expected of such a system. But the design was accepted, possibly due, to some extent, to the expected low cost. Once the system is in operation, however, the deficiencies are recognized and efforts are made to correct them. That approach often results in a total cost that would not have been approved in the beginning.

This situation is perhaps most common in the construction of a public project. The original bid comes in at a certain figure, but change orders soon escalate the cost several hundred percent. Although inflation is usually blamed for the substantial increase, it is usually caused by adding certain essential features and perhaps some frills that had been left out of the original request.

We have all heard of the relative difficulty of finding programmers who are willing to spend their time maintaining existing computer programs. It seems that most programmers would rather spend their time creating something new. Newly hired programmers can often expect to be broken in on maintenance work.

Rather than spend an inordinate amount of time trying to find such people, can a company do something to reduce the amount of maintenance programming needed? Yes, there are some techniques that will help to accomplish that. One is to exercise a little more control over users and their constant requests for changes. You might decide to charge them for any changes made at their request. Certainly the requirement that their requests are subject to a careful study by a review committee may cause them to be more cautious and objective.

Another approach is to control programmers more strictly. Make a review of recent program changes to see if any patterns emerge. For example, does there seem to be a concentration of changes relative to a certain programmer or to a certain technique? As an example, one computer programmer wrote all his programs so that any variable data required for execution had to be entered from punched cards instead of from the computer console typewriter. While it had been known all along that the punched card method would be inferior, the programmer proceeded to provide for the data that way. The cause of such a problem can be determined without great effort. See if it can be alleviated by some additional training or perhaps by using a technique that may take more effort at design time but reduces the effort needed later.

GETTING STARTED

As an organization is about to begin its first EDP audit, it is faced with the serious question of how or where to obtain the service. It is unlikely that the venture will be successful if a financial auditor inexperienced in EDP is appointed to perform the function.

If the need for an EDP audit is sporadic rather than continuous, the most common solution is to hire someone for each audit project on a consulting basis. The service could be obtained from a CPA firm or consulting business specializing in that type of work.

At some point, mainly depending on the extent of EDP operations, the decision may be made to appoint a full-time auditor. If the company decides to hire an experienced EDP auditor, numerous problems might be avoided. On the other hand, if the company opts to hire an outsider (or make an internal transfer), with the intent of giving that person additional training to make him or her an EDP auditor, a crucial decision has to be made: should it select an EDP specialist and train that person in auditing, or should it select a financial auditor and train that person in EDP topics?

There is no doubt that to be successful in EDP auditing, a person must have the qualities of both of those positions. To be good at EDP, one must have a logical mind, be creative, and be able to do detail work. To be a good financial auditor, one must be naturally inquiring (if not nosy), understand overall operations and appreciate what has an impact on the bottom line, and be able to make suggestions for improvements.

Considering how much disagreement there still is on this point, apparently there is no clear-cut answer as to which is the better route; essentially, the choice still boils down to personalities. However, since EDP audits seem to become more and more complex in a technical rather than financial sense, it would appear that EDP knowledge is becoming the more important qualification.

PROFESSIONAL ORGANIZATIONS

Several organizations are devoting portions of their educational programs to the topic of EDP auditing. Examples are the American Institute of Certified Public Accountants (AICPA), the Data Processing Management Association (DPMA), and the Institute of Internal Auditors (IIA).

An organization that is totally dedicated to EDP auditing is the EDP Auditors Association. Founded in 1969, the EDPAA now has 3,500 members in 34 chapters in 8 countries throughout the world. The main objective of this association is to foster EDP auditing education among auditors, data processing specialists, users, and management. Its chapters have the typical monthly meetings, along with sponsoring regional conferences. The highlight of the year is the Annual International Conference, scheduled for Mexico City in June 1980 and Washington, D.C. in June 1981. Administrative offices are located at 7016 Edgebrook Lane, Hanover Park, Illinois 60103.

A separate, but affiliated, organization, namely, the EDP Auditors Foundation, has been established to handle education and research matters. Major publications to date are the periodical *The EDP Auditor* and the book *Control Objectives*.

CERTIFICATION OF DATA PROCESSING AUDITORS

Over the years, various professional organizations have established certification programs for members of their fields. Relevant examples are the certification programs for public accountants (CPA), data processors (CDP), management accountants (CMA), and internal auditors (CIA).

A certification program for EDP auditors (Certified Data Processing Auditor, CDPA) went into effect on July 1, 1978.

Phase I of the program, which lasted for one year, was to certify those EDP auditors by virtue of their work experience. Phase II, which went into effect July 1, 1979, requires that an applicant pass an examination in addition to meeting the experience requirement.

A feature of this program is that a holder is obligated to satisfy continuing education requirements in order to maintain certification. The program is under the direction of the EDP Auditors Foundation, 7016 Edgebrook Lane, Hanover Park, Illinois 60103.

One test of the value of a certification program is its impact upon the hiring of applicable professionals. It will be interesting to watch how quickly the requirement of a CDPA shows up in help-wanted advertisements for data processing auditors.

Glossary

accuracy the degree of freedom from error; will vary considerably depending on the interaction of people and machines.

alphanumeric a field of data that contains alphabetic and numeric characters, such as a street address.

anticipation control a control based on the expectation that a certain transaction will occur by a certain time; if it does not, this indicates a potential problem.

audit the process of examining procedures in order to draw a conclusion about their reliability.

audit program a computer program used by an auditor to reprocess client data.

audit trail that portion of a system that permits one to trace forward from source documents to accounting results or trace backward from accounting results to source documents. May also be called *management trail* or *transaction trail*, since its use is not restricted to auditing.

authorization a right provided by management to selected individuals to allow them to approve transactions, procedures, or total systems.

backup a secondary file, piece of hardware, or procedure that can be used if the primary one is no longer available.

batch processing collecting a number of transactions and processing them as a group. For instance, computerized payroll systems typically use batch processing.

batch total a numeric total of a specific field of data. Used to ensure that every record in the batch is processed in the correct amount.

block diagram obsolete for program flowchart.

bonding obtaining an insurance policy to reimburse a firm for losses due to theft or certain other conditions caused by employees.

branch in computer programming, a conditional statement that causes the computer to go to one of several alternative points in a program for the next instruction to be executed.

bug an error in a program or system.
card punch a machine used to enter source data on punched cards. Typically called a *keypunch*.
character a digit, a letter, or a special symbol such as $, ?, or *.
checkpoint that point in a procedure where an interruption can occur without creating the need to go back to the beginning.
COBOL acronym for *C*ommon *B*usiness *O*riented *L*anguage; a programming language most appropriate for handling business files.
compare a programming step that relates one condition or field of data to another. The outcome of the comparison determines the next step the computer will perform.
compensating control a control that makes up for the absence of another.
compiler a program that converts a high-level program to machine language so that it can be executed by the computer.
compliance audit an audit whose purpose is to determine if certain procedures were followed.
connector a symbol on a flowchart that is used to connect one diagram or segment to another, often on another sheet of paper.
control a method used either to cause operations to work as planned or to measure the deviation from the plan.
control clerk a person whose duties focus on accurate and efficient processing of data. May work within or outside the computer center.
conversion a change in methods, machines, or languages.
core a form of electronic storage used in the central processing unit of a computer.
counter a programming term for that portion of a program which accumulates a total.
data base a number of data files and their interrelationships.
data coding determining the account number or other identifier that distinguishes one transaction from another, and writing the code on a source document and/or entering it to the computer on a keyboard.
debug to locate and remove errors from a computer program.
digit a numeric character.
direct access see random access.
disc a form of computer secondary storage that permits direct access to records in the file.
display unit an output unit that shows data visually on a screen instead of printing data on paper.
documentation all the records indicating how a system was designed and how it is to be operated.
down time the period during which a system or a machine is not available for service because of mechanical or other problems.
dump see file dump.

GLOSSARY

echo check an automatic computer process that sends data back to a previous point to check for a possible error in transmission.
edit to review for errors. Performed by humans or computers.
EDP abbreviation for *electronic data processing*.
erase to wipe out or destroy. Since most data are eventually erased, care must be taken to ensure that erasure doesn't happen prematurely.
external storage data storage outside the computer, such as magnetic tapes or disks. Also called *secondary storage*.
field a unit of data, such as clock number or hours worked.
file a collection of similar records, such as for employees, on a reel of magnetic tape or a disc. May be detail, master, current-balance, or year-to-date, for example.
file dump a printout of the contents of a file for manual review.
file label an internal or external label or code used to identify a file to a person or to a computer.
file maintenance the process of updating a file either to correct errors or to make changes, such as updating addresses or the number of dependents in a payroll system.
flowchart a graphical representation of an overall EDP system or of the logic of a computer program.
fraud in the context of EDP systems, any attempt to wrongfully take something from an employer or a fellow employee through manipulation of a business system.
hard copy output that appears on a sheet of paper. Hard copy is particularly helpful in establishing an audit trail.
hardware the equipment portion of a computer operation.
hardware monitor a device used to check computer components. Used to determine if there is a proper mix of devices and relevant speeds.
hash total a verification method that uses a numeric field whose total is not otherwise of any significance, such as a total of part numbers.
input data and/or instructions to be entered into a computer.
instruction coding writing program steps for eventual execution by the computer.
integrated test facility a test program that processes "live" transactions in such a way that valid files are not disturbed. The method involves creating data for a fictitious "minicompany" that are then processed, together with regular data, on the system to be tested.
internal audit a system audit by a designated employee rather than by an external auditor.
key a field of data typically used to sort data into a relevant order.
keypunch to punch holes into punch cards for the purpose of entering data into a computer. Also refers to a card punch.

key-verify to check the accuracy of keypunching by entering the data a second time for comparison to their first entry.
library the physical location where data are stored. Usually has restricted access to enhance control.
limit check a test to see if a value falls within specified bounds.
log a record of what processing has taken place. May be prepared by humans or the machine.
logic the relationship of steps that will produce a desired result.
loop flowchart or program steps that are repeated a number of times.
machine language the detailed language into which programs and data must be translated in order to be executed by the computer.
magnetic core one form of electronic storage used in the central processing unit of a computer.
magnetic tape a form of secondary storage (and hence also input and output) which is accessed sequentially.
mainframe the central processing unit of a computer.
master file a file whose data are semipermanent. Usually processed in conjunction with a transaction file.
memory storage, either primary in the central processing unit or one of several secondary forms outside the computer.
minicompany see integrated test facility.
monitor see hardware monitor and software monitor.
off-line a device or a process neither attached to nor under current control of the computer, such as a keypunch machine.
on-line a device or process that is attached to or under the control of the computer, such as a disc drive.
overflow a condition whereby a value becomes too large to fit in a specified area in storage. The overflow amount is usually lost unless it is immediately detected and appropriately handled.
parallel operation running a present system and a new system (a replacement) side by side. Generally, the goal is to see if the new system can do a satisfactory job.
parallel simulation processing actual data again by a specially prepared program. The objective is to determine if results are similar to those produced by the regular program.
parity an electronic, self-checking feature built into computers and certain secondary storage devices. The purpose of the feature is to assure that the machine itself does not make any errors by adding or dropping magnetic charge.
performance evaluation an analysis of how well a function is being performed. May be applied by managers or by auditors.
preventive maintenance the process of attending to equipment in such a way as to prevent a breakdown.
program a set of instructions provided to a computer.
program flowchart a diagram that shows the logic used to set up the steps in writing a program.

GLOSSARY

program list a printout of the instructions in a program. Helpful in the debugging process.

programming language a collection of words and terms that can be used to code the instructions of a program.

punch card a card with holes punched in particular positions that is used to store data for computer use. One of several forms of secondary storage.

random access a processing method whereby data can be obtained from a file directly, without the need for the computer to search through the whole file to get what is needed. Also called *direct access*. Typical of a disk file, as opposed to magnetic tape, which allows only sequential access.

read a programming step that causes a computer to accept data from some input device such as a magnetic tape drive.

real-time processing processing of transactions as they occur, as in an airline reservation system.

record a collection of the fields of data relevant to a particular account, customer, employee, or the like.

record count a control that assures that the number of records in a file remains constant.

redundancy information that is strictly unnecessary but that may aid in ensuring accuracy. For example, recording both a clock number and several characters of an employee's name, though redundant, reduces the chance that subsequent steps will process an incorrect account.

rerun to run a program again because of an error or other problem in the original run.

run to execute a computer program.

run-to-run total a total from one run used to tie into the next. Mainly assures that data are neither gained nor lost and that certain processing steps are consistent.

secondary storage data storage outside the computer, as on magnetic tape. Opposed to primary storage, such as magnetic core, in the central processing unit.

self-checking digit a digit appended to the code which identifies a transaction. Used to determine automatically if the code is valid.

sequence check a test to determine whether data are in the proper sequence.

sequential access obtaining records from a file by searching through the file sequentially until the the desired items are found.

signal a sentinel, such as that used at the end of a data file. This is the means whereby the computer program determines that there are no more data.

software computer programs and related aids.

software monitor special program steps used to check application programs for efficient use.

sort to place in sequence, either manually or by machine.
source document a form that generally represents the first recording of data.
standard a value or amount against which actual transactions are judged.
storage a place where programs and data reside, as in core memory or on magnetic tape.
storage cell a storage location in the central processing unit of a computer. Capable of holding a certain number of characters, depending on the design of the machine.
substantive audit an audit whose purpose is to check for the quality of data.
system the interrelationship of people, machines, data, and processes in handling an application.
system flowchart a diagram that shows the flow of data among people and machines.
terminal a device that can be used for input and/or output. Typically includes a keyboard for input and a printer or a cathode ray tube for output.
throughput the amount of data that can be processed in a given period of time. Generally far more important than a quoted input, output, or processing speed.
transaction trail see audit trail.
update to bring a file up to date with current activity.
verify to check for accuracy, as in key verification of punched cards.

Supplementary Readings

BOOKS AND PAMPHLETS

Audit and Evaluation of Computer Security. Washington, D.C.: National Bureau of Standards, 1977. This represents the proceedings of a three-day workshop attended by 82 participants representing government and business.

Computer Audit Guidelines. Toronto: Canadian Institute of Chartered Accountants, 1975. This book describes what to look for in an EDP audit. Designed to be used in conjunction with *Computer Control Guidelines* (see next title), it has become the basis for five-day auditing courses.

Computer Control Guidelines. Toronto: Canadian Institute of Chartered Accountants, 1970. This publication remains the standard treatment of the minimum standards of internal control in a computer-based data processing system. It is the basis for three-day control courses held throughout Canada and the United States.

Control Objectives, second edition. Hanover Park, Ill.: EDP Auditors Foundation for Education and Research, 1977. Details the purpose of various controls and describes what an auditor can do to verify that they exist.

Courtney, Robert H., Jr. *Security Risk Assessment in EDP Systems*, revised edition. Poughkeepsie, N.Y.: IBM, 1975. Details a very effective way to quantify decisions involving computer security.

Davis, Gordon B. *Auditing and EDP*. New York: American Institute of Certified Public Accountants, 1968. A very readable text whose topics are still relevant.

Effective Methods of EDP Quality Assurance. Wellesley, Mass.: Q.E.D. Information Sciences, 1977.

Enger, Norman L. *Management Standards for Developing Information Systems*. New York: AMACOM, 1976. Provides many ideas for the successful development of EDP systems.

Forty-two Suggestions for Improving Security in Data Processing Operations. White Plains, N.Y.: IBM, 1973.

Fifty-four Ways to Reduce DP Costs. Pennsauken, N.J.: Auerbach, 1976. A collection of cost-cutting measures taken by 180 users surveyed by Auerbach.

Greenwood, Frank, and Lee A. Gagnon. *Assessing Computer Center Effectiveness*. New York: AMACOM, 1977. Furnishes many ideas that both management and auditors may find useful.

Jancura, Elise G., *Computers: Auditing and Control*, second edition. New York: Mason/Charter, 1977. A collection of articles that appeared in various periodicals.

Jancura, Elise G., and Arnold H. Berger. *Computers: Auditing and Control*. New York: Mason/Charter, 1973. A collection of articles that appeared in various periodicals.

Mair, William C., Donald R. Wood, and Keagle W. Davis. *Computer Control and Audit*. Altamonte Springs, Florida: The Institute of Internal Auditors, 1976. A very practical discussion about the topic of EDP auditing. Designed more for the practitioner than for the student.

Martin, James. *Security, Accuracy, and Privacy in Computer Systems*. Englewood Cliffs, N.J.: Prentice-Hall, 1973.

Parker, Donn B. *Crime by Computer*. New York: Scribner & Sons, 1976.

Porter, W. Thomas, and William E. Perry. *EDP Controls and Auditing*, second edition. Belmont, California: Wadsworth, 1977. A textbook designed specifically for the college student or others who want to learn about the field. Contains case studies and excellent end-of-chapter problems.

Systems Auditability and Control. Altamonte Springs, Florida: The Institute of Internal Auditors, 1977. Consists of three volumes: an Executive Report, a Control Practices Report, and an Audit Practices Report. Describes systems control and audit practices in use. Generally referred to as the *SAC Report*.

RECOMMENDED PERIODICALS

Data Processing Digest. Reports on articles appearing in over 200 periodicals.

EDP Auditing. A loose-leaf service provided by Auerbach Publishers, Pennsauken, N.J.

The EDP Auditor. A technical journal published quarterly by the EDP Auditors Foundation for Education and Research.

EDP Auditor Update. This bimonthly publication covers the activities of the EDP Auditors Association.

EDPACS (EDP AUDIT, Control & Security). An excellent how-to publication on all aspects of computer controls and auditing.

SELECTED ARTICLES OF SPECIFIC INTEREST

Allen, Brandt. "The Biggest Computer Frauds: Lessons for CPA's." *The Journal of Accountancy*, May 1977.

Allen, John Robert. "The Auditor's Relationship to the Development of Data Processing Controls." *Management Accounting*, November 1977.

Anderson, R. J. "Computer Controls." *The Internal Auditor*, April 1976.

Barnett, Arnold. "Securing User Involvement." *Journal of Data Management*, January 1978.

Bell, Thomas E. "Twenty-one Money Saving Questions." *Management Controls*, May/June 1977.

"Can Accountants Uncover Management Fraud?" *Business Week*, July 10, 1978.

Clinch, J. Houston M., Jr., and Charles E. Johnston. "Auditing EDP Efficiency." *Bank Administration*, May 1977.

Cooke, Lawrence H., Jr. "Perfect Chargeout Just Not Obtainable." *Computerworld*, October 17, 1977.

Dyba, Jerome E. "To Edit or Not to Edit." *Journal of Systems Management*, April 1974.

Fitzgerald, Robert. "Organizing for an EDP Internal Audit." *Journal of Systems Management*, September 1978.

Horwitz, Geoff. "Needed: A Computer Audit Philosophy." *The Journal of Accountancy*, April 1976.

"How to Get Started in Performance Evaluation." *EDP Performance Review*, June 1977.

Kirkley, John L. "A Scathing Look at U.S. Standards." *Datamation*, June 1978.

Lowe, Ronald L. "Auditing the Corporate Information System." *The CPA Journal*, November 1977.

MacNab, Seaforth. "Debugging the EDP Auditor." *The Internal Auditor*, February 1979.

McLaughlin, R. A. "The (MIS) Use of EDP in Government Agencies." *Datamation*, July 1978.

Perry, William E. "The Internal Audit Mandate in EDP." *Chartered Accountant*, September 1977.

Perry, William E., and Jerry FitzGerald. "Designing for Auditability." *Datamation*, August 1977.

Philo, Philip. "The Savings Game." *Management Accounting*, February 1970.

Rittenberg, Larry E., and Gordon B. Davis. "The Roles of Internal and External Auditors in Auditing EDP Systems." *The Journal of Accountancy*, December 1977.

Rolefson, Jerome F. "The DP Check-Up." *Journal of Systems Management*, November 1978.

Roussey, Robert S. "Third-Party Review of the Computer Service Center." *Journal of Accountancy*, August 1978.

Toellner, John. "Performance Measurement in Systems and Programming." *Infosystems*, December 1977/January 1978.

"User Ratings of Software Packages." *Datamation*, each December issue.

Welling, Priscilla. "Introducing the MISA (MIS Auditor)." *Management Accounting*, February 1977.

Index

accounts-payable systems, 132
accuracy, of EDP system, 7, 10–12
  in computer center auditing, 174–175
  in data generation and conversion auditing, 146–150
  in file generation, 170–171
  in preinstallation activities audit, 55–57
  in program development activities audit, 122–124
  in system development activities audit, 84–87
American Institute of Certified Public Accountants (AICPA), 92, 190
American National Standards Institute (ANSI), flowchart symbols of, 97
"annotation" symbol, 105
ANSI, *see* American National Standards Institute
auditors
  certification of, 190–191
  EDP, hiring, 189
  system development role of, 92–93
audit programs, 30
audit trail, 81–82
authorization of transactions, 130–133

backup
  data, 82–83
  equipment, 83
  files, 24
  procedure, 83–84
  program, 83
  security controls and, 163–165
batch entry
  conversion to, from on-line entry, 130
  data submission periods in, 135–136
batch total, as program control, 113–115, 143, 170

bonding, 17, 166
Business Automation (magazine), 146
business information systems, raw data for, 67

CDPA (Certified Data Processing Auditor), 190–191
Census Bureau, U.S., 1
centralized processing, 53
central processing unit (CPU), 45
certification, of data processing auditors, 190–191
Certified Data Processing Auditor (CDPA), 190–191
change committees, 186
checklists, 148, 150
checkpoint, 12–13, 175
committees
  change, 186
  steering, 34–38, 50–52
computer(s)
  editing of, 24
  initiation of transactions by, 78
  reruns, 177–178
  specialists used for design of, 91–92
  see also EDP systems; hardware; software
computer centers
  auditing, 173–184
  authorization of employees in, 132
  control departments in, 145
  controls in, 161–173
  documentation for, 159–161
  efficiency in, 13–14
  fraud by programmers in, 125–126
  goals of, 155–158
  standards for, 158–159
Congress, U.S., Foreign Corrupt Practices Act (1977) of, 5
controls, of computers
  audit trail and, 81–82
  backups and, 82–84
  classifications of, 23–25
  cost-benefit considerations of, 3
  in data generation, 140–145
  design of system and, 3–4, 80–81
  efficiency, 166–168
  forms, 131

in hardware, 117–118, 161–162
input/output, 162, 180
legal requirements for, 5
in maintenance of systems and programs, 187–189
overdoing, 4–5
positive/negative, 24–25
in preinstallation activities, 50–52
of problem definition, 80
in program development process, 107–119
SAC report on, 5–6
security, 88–89, 163–166
software, 107–108
source, 11, 129–130
in system conversion, 77–78
see also EDP audits
conversion, data, *see* data generation and conversion
conversion of files, 168–171
corrective controls, 24
cost-effectiveness
  of accuracy in EDP systems, 12
  of change, 186–187
  of computer controls, 3, 4
  of data conversion process, 149
costs, data-processing
  billing users for, 167–168
  in computer centers, 175–176
  overtime and, 177
  in preinstallation activities, 34, 44
  of security controls, 163–164
  standards and, 49
CPU (central processing unit), 45
customer base, erosion of, 26

data
  backup, 82–83
  coding, 129
  loss of, before programming, 135
  in program testing, 103–104
  proprietary, protection of, 8
  raw, for business information systems, 67
  retention of, 138
  source, 11, 68

data (cont.)
  in systems operation, 68–69
  test, auditing method, 121
  see also data generation and conversion
data base systems, 53–54
data conversion, *see* data generation and conversion
data generation and conversion
  auditing, 146–154
  controls in, 140–145
  documentation in, 139–140
  goals of, 128–129
  procedures for, 133–138
  standards in, 129–130
  transaction authorization and, 130–133
Datamation (magazine), 101*n*
Data Processing Management Association (DPMA), 190
data processing systems, *see* EDP systems
debugging, of computer programs, 99
  error types and, 101–102
  program tests and, 102–104
design, of EDP systems, *see* EDP system development
detective controls, 24
disaster plans, for computer centers, 179–180
distributed processing, 53
documentation
  barriers to, 74–75
  for control centers, 159–161, 173–174
  in data generation and conversion, 139–140
  of manpower estimates, 87
  of preinstallation activities, 46
  in program development, 104–106
  in system development, 72–75, 79–80
  of systems analysis, 27
  see also flowchart(s)
DPMA (Data Processing Management Association), 190
dual read control, 118
duplication, testing by computer for, 111

edit programs, 98
  as program control, 115–117
EDP Auditors Association (EDPAA), 190
EDP Auditors Foundation, 190

EDP audits
  audit trails in, 81–82
  of data generation and conversion, 146–154
  implementing, 189–190
  objectives of, 26–27
  of preinstallation activities, 54–66
  problems with, 3–6, 31–32
  of program development activities, 119–127
  standards for, 22–23
  strategy of, 27–29
  techniques for, 30–31
  topic selection in, 25–26
  types of, 6–9
  see also control, of computers
EDP systems
  development of, 1, 69–84
  operation of, day-to-day, 67–69
  see also computer(s); EDP audits; hardware; software
effectiveness, of EDP system, 7, 20
  in computer center, 182–183
  in preinstallation activities considerations, 63–66
  of programs, 127
  in systems development activities auditing, 89–91
efficiency, of EDP system, 7, 12–14
  in computer center audits, 175–178
  controls of, 166–168
  of data generation and conversion, 150–152
  leasing vs. buying decision and, 58, 60–62
  in program development activities auditing, 124–125
  in system development activities auditing, 87
electronic data processing systems, *see* EDP systems
employee(s)
  in computer center, 20
  control in programming and, 118–119
  development, 183
  efficiency of, 150–151
  and internal auditors, 7, 13
  part-time, 57
  problem definition by, 80
  security controls and, 165–166
  teaching, about EDP systems, 36
  see also programmers, computer

208 INDEX

equipment, computer, *see* hardware
Equity Funding fraud case, 153, 181
error(s)
    correction, 137–138
    detection of, 140–145
    edit programs and, 98, 115–117
    in preinstallation phase, 55–57
    preventing, through system design, 11–12, 20, 161
    programming, types of, 101–102
    recording, 146–148
    statistics, 130
external audits
    by CPA firms, 6
    fraud detection in, 14
    objectives of, 27
    by taxing bodies, 6–7

feasibility studies, in preinstallation activities, 42–45
file(s)
    backup, 24
    comparison to, of transactions, 112
    conversion of, 168–171
    documentation, 46
    dumps, 30–31
    protection of, 171–173
file protect ring, 172–173
flowchart(s)
    accuracy reflected in, 56–59, 86
    fraudulent logic in, 14–16
    print layout forms and, 123
    program, 97, 105–106
    security controls on, 88
Foreign Corrupt Practices Act (1977), U.S., 5
forms
    checklist, 148, 150
    design, 129
    input, 136–137
    prenumbered, for input control, 143
    print layout, 123
    transaction authorization and, 131
fraud, in EDP system, 8, 14–17
    in computer center auditing, 180–182
    in data generation and conversion, 153

in preinstallation activities consideration, 62–63
prevention of, 17–19, 161
in program development activities auditing, 125–126
in systems development activities auditing, 87–88

General Accounting Office (GAO), U.S., 49
generalized audit software packages, 119–120
goals
    audit, 26–27
    of computer centers, 155–158
    of data generation and conversion, 128–129
    maintenance, 186
    preinstallation, 33–34
    in program development, 96–97
    of system development, 69–71

hardware
    backup, 83
    controls, built-in, 117–118, 161–162
    costs of, 175–176
    for data conversion, 144
    leasing of, 58, 60–62
    monitors, 178
    standards in, 49
    usage levels of, 13
hash totals, 170
Hollerith, Herman, 1

IBM, 1, 5
IIA, *see* Institute of Internal Auditors
Infosystems (magazine), 146
initiation of transactions, 78
input/output control groups, 162, 180
input/output devices, speed of, 45
Institute of Internal Auditors (IIA), 92, 190
    Systems Auditability and Control (SAC) report of, 5–6, 64, 65
instruction codes, 102
integrated test facility (ITF), 183–184
internal audits, 7–8
    objectives of, 27
internal labels, 173
Internal Revenue Service (IRS)
    audits of EDP activities by, 6–7
    data retention ruling by, 138

IRS, *see* Internal Revenue Service
ITF (integrated test facility), 183–184

job rotation, as security control, 18–19, 165–166

keypunching, record combination in, 152
key verification, 24, 143
    conversion errors and, 147–149
    machine, operation of, 149

labels, internal, 173
languages, programming
    nonstandard, 49
    in program development standards, 98–99
leasing vs. buying decision, for computer hardware, 58, 60–62
logic
    errors in, 101–102
    in fraud, 14–16
    program, 31
logs
    console, 174
    fraud prevention through, 182
    transmittal, 143

machine-rated speeds, 57
maintenance, system and program
    controls in, 187–189
    goals of, 186
    standards for, 186–187
management
    auditing standards set by, 22
    computer centers and, 155–156
    of data base system, 53–54
    documentation responsibility and, 75
    fraud prevention planning by, 17–18
    in system design, 92–93
    trail, 81–82
    transaction initiation decisions made by, 78
managers
    of computer centers, 13, 35–36
    leases vs. buy decisions by, 61

INDEX 211

manpower estimates, 87
mark sensing, 137
minicompany approach, 183–184
minicomputers, 52–53
monitors
   hardware, 178
   software, 125
multiprogramming, 45

National Bureau of Standards (NBS), 161–162, 165

on-line entry, 134
   conversion to, from batch entry, 130
overflow control, 118
overrides, manual, 78–79
overtime, costs of, 177

parallel simulation, auditing method, 121–122, 123
parity check, 117–118
Patrick, Robert, 161–162
Performance Assurance and Data Integrity Practices (NBS), 161–162
performance reviews, of EDP system, 8
preinstallation phase of computer system implementation
   auditing of, 54–66
   controls in, 50–52
   data base systems considered in, 53–54
   documentation in, 46
   feasibility studies in, 42–45
   goals in, 33–34
   minicomputers considered in, 52–53
   preliminary surveys in, 38–42
   standards setting in, 46–50
   steering committee used in, 34–38
preliminary surveys, *see* surveys, preliminary
preventive controls, 24
print layout forms, 123
privacy, 8
procedures of EDP system, 7–8
   backup of, 83–84
   standards for, 21
program backup, 83

program development
  auditing, 119–127
  controls in, 107–119
  debugging software in, 99, 101–104
  documentation in, 104–106
  goals in, 96–97
  program writing in, 99–101
  standards in, 97–99
  steps in, 94
  see also programming; software
programmers, computer, 96
  debugging by, 106
  fraud practised by, 14–17, 125–126
  maintenance work and, 188
  overrides by, 78–79
programming
  edits in, 98
  flowcharts in, 97
  languages, 98–99
  writing of programs in, 99–101
  see also program development; software
programs, computer, *see* software
program testing, *see* testing

raw data generation, *see* data generation and conversion
reasonableness checks, 108–109, 142
record counts, 113
  in file conversion, 170
redundant information, 141
reprocessing, auditing method, 121–122, 123
reruns, 177–178
return on investment, as system development goal measurement, 70–71
Revenue Ruling 71-20 (IRS), 138
risk analysis, 163–164

SAC report, *see* Systems Auditability and Control
security, of EDP systems, 8, 19–20
  in computer center auditing, 178–180
  controls, 163–166
  in data generation and conversion, 153–154

in preinstallation activities considerations, 63
in program development activities auditing, 126–127
in systems development auditing, 88–89
self-checking digit, 109–111, 140–141
sequence checking, 113
sign-off procedures, 77
simulation, parallel, 121–122, 123
software
  audit, generalized, 119–120
  authorization by, 131–132
  debugging of, 99, 101–104
  documentation in, 104–106
  monitors, 125
  multiprogramming and, 45
  reviewing, as auditing method, 122
  writing programs and, 99–101
  see also programming
SRI International, 5
standards
  auditing, 22–23
  for computer centers, 158–159
  for maintenance, 186–187
  performance, 21–22
  in preinstallation activities, 46–50
  procedural, 21
  in program development, 97–99
  in system development, 76–80
Stanford Research Institute, 5
steering committee
  as control, 50–52
  in preinstallation activities, 34–38
strategy, audit, formulation of, 27–29
surveys, preliminary, 39–42
  computer capabilities considered in, 38–39
symbols, on flowchart, 97
  "annotation," 105
system design, *see* system development
system development
  auditing, 84–91
  controls in, 80–84
  documentation in, 72–75
  goals in, 69–71

system development (cont.)
  personnel involved in, 91–93
  standards in, 76–80
systems analysts
  data generation and conversion by, 129
  documentation by, 27
Systems Auditability and Control (SAC) report, 5–6, 64, 65

techniques, auditing, 30–31
  favorite, as pitfall, 31
test data method, for auditing program development, 121
test decks, 30, 103, 123
testing
  for duplicates, 111
  for excessive activity, 111–112
  integrated test facility in, 183–184
  program, methods of, 102–104
topics, audit, selection of, 25–26
training, in EDP systems
  computer center documentation used for, 159–160
  continued, of EDP auditor, 64
  deficiencies in, 134–135
  of employees rather than outsiders, 36, 37
transaction(s)
  activity, testing for excessive, 111–112
  authorization, 130–133
  comparison of, to file, 112
  trail, 81–82
turnaround documents, 136

unit record systems, 152
"User Ratings of Software Packages" (*Datamation*), 101*n*
users, computer
  billing, for computer center services, 167–168
  data control responsibility of, 145
  effectiveness of computer center and, 182–183
  and programmers, 96
  in system design, 91–93

vacations, mandatory, as security control, 165
validity checks, 118